21st Century Selling: How to Sell More in Any Climate

Contents

What This Book is and is Not

It is getting harder and harder to get to see, pitch and get answers from prospective clients. Competitors seem to be offering more for a lot less. Clients want more for a lot less. Competing with all of the messages they are getting on a constant basis squeezed into their already packed day is getting exponentially more difficult. Everyone wants everything for nothing and they expect it now and whenever they demand it. Or maybe it's just me!

It doesn't have to be like that; you can make your life a lot easier and more successful and separate yourself from all that noise and hassle. You can have a different conversation, fight different battles, ones which take place on your terms and within your control. You can be the only one left standing when it comes to the client's decision being made. You can have pitches which do not revolve around price.

Sounds wonderful, huh? This has been a reality for me and many others for years. All it takes are a few simple shifts and a different way of thinking; a different approach which produces radically different results. This book will show you how to make your sales life easier and how to sell more.

Everyone these days is a salesperson, but there is a difference between a headmaster selling prospective parents on his or her school and a professional salesperson closing a $10 million integrated software management system to Fujitsu! Both are sales but both use very different skills.

This book is written for professional salespeople who sell either to businesses or to other professionals. It is not to say that every salesperson, like a headmaster, would not benefit from this book, they would—it is just that it is primarily geared to professional and business-to-business salespeople. So if that is you, then read on!

I know that there are a lot of sales books out there offering the latest and greatest ways of closing deals, selling more, selling without pestering and selling in the brave new world. I have read many of them and I will recommend a few as we go along, as some of them are excellent.

The difference in the material that I teach you here is that I am assuming that you instinctively already know how to sell; whether you know it or not you have been selling your whole life. If you are a professional who sells then you know the basics, you know when you are a painful salesperson to be with and I also bet that you instinctively know when you are pushing too hard or not closing hard enough. This is not a "do the basics" and here-they-are book.

What you will learn here, however, is how to close more deals through educational selling, through selling for the 21st century way, letting go of old industry beliefs which just don't work anymore and taking on some new concepts which work in the real world—in today's markets.

The business world has absolutely changed over the last 20 years, and the people you sell to expect you to know your craft and apply it diligently. They already expect you to know your product, your industry and your competitors, and they absolutely do not expect to be sold to in an old fashioned beat-them-until-they-submit way. Your job is to adapt to how the market has changed and sell accordingly.

There are some new skills you are going to have to develop which may have lain dormant up until now, and there are some skills you will also have to tamp down as they may not be so relevant anymore.

There is a lot to this book but if you are after a bit of a summary in order to see what it covers then here you go! This book covers a lot more than these areas but the main thrust of it is this. You will learn:

- How to make yourself the only option on the table.
- How to make sure you do not sell on price.
- How to blow away your competition either as an incumbent or as a predator.
- How to sell to an educated audience.
- How to sell in a changing and developing climate.
- What to do to develop the right relationship at the right time.
- How to find out who to sell to.
- The top five things you need to prospect in today's market.
- When to walk away and when to keep going.
- Who should you be spending most of your time with, and why?
- What skills you need to be the best and stay there?
- How to run an effective sales team and what it means to hire the right people.

I have structured this book in a logical format and essentially it comes in three distinct sections:

Section 1 - How to get in front of the right people - covers the educational sales process from start to finish, starting with prospecting and moving through to face to face meetings, then to presenting, then to developing the relationship and then closing the deal. This section also covers how to maximise your time and how to organise your educational information so you don't have to do the same things over and over.

I do not cover the basics; for example, how to pick up the phone and how to start a conversation. There are plenty of books which do that far better than I can. I also won't patronise you by teaching you that you have to ask for the deal and find the decision maker—as I said earlier I assume you already know how to sell. I am only using the process as this is the easiest way to cover what needs to be covered in the most logical format I could think of.

Section 2 - How to set up the deal and close it - covers how to secure and solidify what you do and how to get more for less after the initial prospecting is done. Essentially it covers what you need to know from creating a long lasting relationship to developing your pipeline so you do not have to pick up the phone cold again.

Section 3 - How to set yourself up for success – this section is all about how to scale what you do from how to find and build an outstanding sales team to how to get everyone else selling for you. It also covers the mental attributes you need to succeed.

Everything I teach you here has been tested and works, and I have personally used these strategies and approaches for over 20 years with outstanding results. This is how the top guys and girls sell and this is how you get results, which are not only for now but for the long term—which is what really matters when you are developing a name for yourself in sales.

How to Get the Most Out of This Book

What most people do is read a book once and then think "that had some good stuff." They then put it down and it never sees the light of day again. Ninety percent of what you read you forget within a few days, and within six months ninety percent of that is also lost. I don't want that to happen to you with this.

There is a lot covered here and I strongly suggest that to get the most out of this book you read it first from cover to cover, highlighting as you go. Then go back and leave a nice review on the site you purchased it from! Then pick out the sections which had most relevance to you and go through them in detail again, making notes on what you are going to do in the next 30 days to make it a must for you to implement the changes you need to make.

Also there will be chapters which will highlight the skills you need to work on more than others, so pick the top three or four and make a plan to develop the skills you need to make educational selling your primary way of winning business.

Basically the message here is read, highlight, re-read, make notes and then create a plan of action which actually induces change and therefore results.

Also I strongly suggest that you test your results, as taking my word for it is not enough. You have to see it working for yourself which then creates belief, which in turn makes you more certain of your results so you will win more business and become a more successful sales professional.

Above all, please enjoy the process, it is meant to be a less pressurised way of selling, a more strategic approach which puts you in control and takes away your competition, not a stressful back to school experience.

So What Qualifies Me to Write This Book?

I have been selling professionally for twenty years and I have built from scratch several very successful technology companies using the information I teach here. I have successfully started and sold companies and I have sold to many of the largest companies and brands in the UK and globally including Saatchi, McLaren, DS Smith, Ring Central, Williams F1, Perceptive Informatics and many others.

I am currently a sales director for a large telecoms carrier and so I am teaching you relevant current methodologies which work, as I used them yesterday and the day before and the day before that! I do not teach sales for a living, I do sales and get results, every day. I teach other salespeople but not as a career, I teach them to further themselves and my businesses. I also teach other sales teams in partner organisations these exact same principles, as many of our sales come through other organisations who sell our services.

I sell to corporates face to face and to other businesses in my industry alike, but the principles remain the same, education, education, education!

I have also been lucky enough in the last 20 plus years to sell everything from jewellery cleaner in a market (which is still to this day one of my favourite experiences in sales) to large land deals in Eastern Europe, to real estate and large multinational technology deals which took years to complete.

The majority of my selling success, however, has been in technology and as you will see many of the stories and experiences I use as examples are from the technology industry. All of the content though is applicable to any professional sale type, so please just make it relevant to you.

I actually started to write this book because time and time again people I work with have very kindly said that I should teach what I do to a wider audience, as in their experience this way of selling is the best they have ever seen, so here it is!

You will see from my style that I am quite direct and to the point and that my writing style is not as free flowing as others. For that I apologise but I wanted to write this myself as you should hear it from me, not from a ghost writer who misses the essence of what needs to be covered. I do try to use humour as often as possible in sales and for some reason I don't seem to be able to convert that to writing so you will just have to take it from me that I am funny face to face!

Section 1

How to Get in Front of the Right People

What is Education Selling and Why Does it Work?

Over the years I have seen so many teachings about selling, many of which boil down to a few salient points:

- Sell features and benefits.
- Listen more than you speak.
- Build a relationship.
- Don't take no for an answer.
- Get to the decision maker.
- It's a numbers game.
- Always get a win-win.

And so on. These are all very good points, and rarely implemented correctly, but none talk about educating your prospective customer to get him in a position of trust so he buys from you. Most salespeople I work with and have seen go to sales meetings with one objective, to get their point across, regardless of whether that point is relevant or not. They are so focused on what they want to say that they really don't actually listen and take in what is happening.

Even the very good salespeople who listen and pay attention and adapt to the fluid situation do fail to grasp one single extremely important point which is, the prospect they are speaking to could not give a flying stuff about what they have to say or what they are discussing unless there is something in it for him, which either relieves an immediate pain he has or makes his job or life better.

You can tell people all the features and benefits you like but if you don't add value to their jobs or businesses then you are wasting your breath.

Educational selling, on the other hand, turns all the previously held truths on their heads and approaches the whole sales process from a completely different angle. Educational selling is a complete mind-set where it is your job to educate your audience.

A great definition of educational based selling is:

"Upgrade your user, not your product. 'Value' is less about the stuff and more about the stuff the stuff enables. Don't build better cameras—build better photographers." — Kathy Sierra

Educational selling allows you to:

- Be more in control of the situation and conversation
- Create credibility with your audience
- Become a trusted advisor over the long term
- Build trust with your prospect
- Build closer relationships far quicker
- Eliminate your competition from the conversation
- Direct the whole conversation away from price
- Close more deals

It will become very apparent how these are all very achievable as we progress. I will give you specific examples so you can see exactly how it works in the real world, so you can apply it to your own product or service.

Educational selling works because you are giving the prospects what they want, the power to make an informed decision, which adds real benefit to them. Benefit they can see and believe and they feel they are in control of. Many decision makers make decisions in a confused state where they only make the decision based on the lowest price or how the salesperson looks.

Your role is to raise them up above all of that poor decision making fog and let them see the way forward through their own eyes. When they do this, they make an informed quality decision which in their own minds is their decision, not based some other salesperson's agenda.

It is not a short term trick or manipulation technique; educational selling is all about integrity and it is all about a genuine belief that you must impart what you know so you can help others get what they want. If you approach it from a selfish or manipulative standpoint then you will be found out and you will appear phoney, and therefore you will fail. You have been warned!

So if you have a genuine desire to help your prospects and clients make better decisions which help them, and you then read on and see how educational selling can transform your sales …

What the Hell Are You Going to Tell Them?

For education selling there are two phases for using it effectively to sell more.

1. Get the best relevant and most interesting data together;
2. Change your approach so you can deliver it in the most effective way possible.

This chapter will deal with what you need to find out about; every other chapter will deal with what you do with that information and how you deliver it.

When did you last do a pitch? What was it like and how did it go? Regardless of the outcome what did you talk about, can you remember? Did you come out with the same old patter you have said for months or years? Has your pitch come about because of experience or have you deliberately sat down and planned what you say every time?

When you pitch, do you wing it or are you very structured? I guess it will largely depend on your audience and your industry but most of the sales pitches I have seen are very dull—same as anyone else's affairs, where no attention is given to the audience and you can tell that it is old, stale and very selfish.

Generally, pitches follow the same lines: this is who we are, this is what we do, these are our products, this is our price and these are our clients.

In fact, even if the pitch is well delivered and fresh, the content is often so poor that the audience is left numb, pretending to fake interest and wishing it was the end. Have you ever sat through one of these meetings or listened to one on the phone? Ever delivered one? I know I have!

From now on your outcome should be that ANYBODY you come into contact with where you are pitching in any way, from a chance meeting at a football game, to a two hour long presentation, to the board room, leaves them thinking, "Wow, that was interesting," "I didn't know that," "I know a lot more about that now than I did before," or, "That guy or girl really knows what he/she is talking about."

In order to move from the old fashioned, "These are our benefits, this is our company profile, this is our price," to the informative, intriguing, value driven pitch, there are certain things you must do:

Gather Your Facts

First, please get away from the whole traditional corporate pitch of, "This is our company, this is the turnover, size, number of employees, etc." Either the audience knows who you are already or they actually don't care yet. It is up to their contracts or other related departments to do due diligence on you when you win the deal, so leave that for later. If they want to ask you, they will. Your credibility will come from your knowledge, not your size.

Please remember that if you work for a small organisation, you can absolutely be the David winning big deals with this way of selling.

First, become educated yourself in your industry—the trends, the facts, the movers and shakers, and the latest up-to-date technologies. You cannot educate anyone else unless you yourself first become educated. As Bobbi Brown of the same name cosmetics label says, "You can't teach if you're not learning."

Without boasting, I would say that I am one of the most knowledgeable people in my industry in the sector I sell in. I am not technical but I have taken a lot of time to really understand what it is that we do technically, and as the technology is quite new, there is a lot to learn. You must be the same, you cannot just know your own product and how it works (mind you, for a lot of people that would be a start!). You must understand your technology, your industry and your audience's industry and how it applies to them.

This is not about technical selling or pre-sales where the techies can run rings around you, this is about getting to know pertinent, relevant, useful information your audience will want to know.

The broader your depth of knowledge, the better your pitch will be, as these days it is nowhere near enough to be only able to sell to a finance director, or operations manager. Organisations expect you to be able to pitch at all levels and through all departments. Even if there is a team of you who sell, become the leader who knows enough to stand his ground on multiple fronts and at all levels.

Let me clarify through an example. Recently I went to see a prospect, and I was talking (pitching) to the managing director. We did our bit, and after I educated him on where things were going in our industry and what was happening, he was ready to take it to the next stage. Now in the past I would have then brought in technical people to talk about that element, and operations people to talk about that element, but as I was now the fountain of all knowledge in his mind, he brought in his chief technical officer and his head of finance, right there and then. There was no time to defer to people in my organisation who know more about these parts of the business than myself. It was irrelevant anyway as all they wanted to know was what I told the MD. They then took that knowledge and applied it to their areas of responsibility. All the key stakeholders were now brought in so the MD was validated for his decision which made everything much, much easier.

Later the details were thrashed out by finance and operations, but by then the deal was done and they were signed. All too often salespeople lean on others in their company to sell for them, either as pre sales or technical sales. Do not let this be you. You have to take responsibility for the whole process. You do not need to learn everything about every bit of detail, but be prepared to learn and get knowledge in all areas or you will get left behind.

So educating yourself first is the key. Every industry is different and so obviously you must adapt to your particular niche, but here are the topics to really get to know:

Your industry:

1. What are the general trends in your industry?
2. What are the top three main trends in your industry?
3. What has happened over the last 12 – 24 months which has changed the landscape?
4. What products are being phased out and which ones are coming up?
5. Who are the movers and shakers, either as companies or individuals? What are they doing, and who are they doing it with?

Your competition:

1. Who are they?
2. Who are your top five competitors?

3. What are they doing in the market that you are not?
4. What differentiates you from them? (I am asked this question all the time.)
5. How large and profitable are they compared to you?

Your product or service:

1. What are the top ways it adds value?
2. Make sure you technically know how it works if you need to.
3. What are the plans for it over the next two years?
4. What separates it from every other product or service like it?

And most important ...

Specific trends for your clients' market:

1. What is happening in their markets?
2. What trends are happening in their industries that they will not know about?
3. How can your industry help them with these trends?
4. How can you find out things about their industries that they will not know about?
5. What are the top things you know about your offering which will help them save money or make more money?

Much of this you will read and probably say to yourself, "Yep, I know this," "This is what I do," and so on. My experience is that this is not the case. The vast majority of sales professionals have a standard patter about their offering and they try to shoe horn that into the situation in front of them. They do not have the breadth of knowledge required to pull off this way of selling.

How much advantage do you believe you could get if you actually researched the above points and learned them inside out and back to front? How knowledgeable would you be with your clients and prospects if you really knew what was happening?

It is time to take a look outside your own company and products to see what is really happening out there. It's time to see who is really doing what, and what changes are happening which will directly affect you and your clients in the next few years. For sure it will continue to change, and you and they will be left behind if you do not step up and educate yourself first.

In the next section I will show you how to organise this information into useful chunks so you can start to plan your sales process. You will need different amounts compiled separately for differing situations. Do not despair, though, as the amount of work to complete it is not that much. I appreciate that as salespeople we all have probably a less than average attention span and attention to detail but for once you need to tap into that part of you that allows you to pay close attention.

Please bear in mind that this information is worth a lot of money to you, so it is well worth taking the time to understand exactly how it works.

You may be wondering where you can find these facts out and how much time and effort is actually required to make this work. There are a couple of answers to this.

To gather specific trends and facts does not have to take that long. There are research companies who will source data for you, but obviously that comes at a price. If you have the budget, then I suggest that you do get a market research company to source and validate the right information.

If you do outsource this part, then you must be specific in what ask for. Ask for say the top three trends over the last five years in your industry, or the figures for the growth in a sector over the last three years. If you do not know what you are looking for, then the bill will grow exponentially.

You cannot outsource your own general education on anything else—only the gathering of facts. No other company will know your industry as well as you, so they will not know what they are looking for as well as you do. What they can do, however, is gather specific facts and data so you can compile it from there. They will probably be better at research than you, but that will be about it. The rest is up to you.

So where do you find out your information from? Here are some ideas. Obviously every industry is different, but these are good places to start:

- Trade journals
- Industry magazines (online and print)
- Trade publications
- Trade blogs
- Industry websites
- University research which is publically available
- Specific industry research (this may cost you but often it is worth it)
- Industry trade shows and exhibitions
- Your competitors' webinars and presentations
- LinkedIn groups and news
- Online newspapers

All too often we do not read the press in our own industry, as the editorial pieces often read like pitches by the companies who advertise, but there is a lot of trend knowledge available in them. I find that reading the two main publications for my industry once a month really helps me understand what is going on, and especially with understanding who is doing what.

If you sell into a specific industry vertical, then you must read their publications and subscribe to them so you know what is happening in their world. We will discuss a lot more later about cross- industry knowledge, however, for now it only makes common sense to know what is important to them. If nothing else, you will come across as having an interest in what they do and you will be able to hold your own in relevant conversations.

You may think this all takes a long time but actually it does not have to.

There are two types of education here: initial fact finding with research to build your pitch, and general ongoing education so you stay ahead of the game and on top of what is going on. The initial part will take the longest to accumulate and organise, but once that is complete you will be most of the way there.

Next we are going to cover how to use the specific information you find about trends and facts on certain interesting aspects of the message you must convey. Knowing it is a start, but using it in a structured way for maximum impact is something quite different.

What Are You Looking For?

There are three areas of information you will need to use, gather and summarise:

1. Your industry
2. Your audience's industry / role or interest
3. Your product or service

As there is so much data available, we need to be able to boil it down into useable chunks. These are some good pointers on what types of information you are looking for:

- Specific interesting facts relating to your audience.
- Specific interesting facts relating to your own industry.
- Trends in your industry which affect your audience.
- Trends in their industry which they will not generally know.
- General market knowledge about your industry.
- General market knowledge about the industry you are selling into.
- Specific interesting things you provide which can make a significant impact.

I generally sell to people in the same industry, so I must know interesting facts relating to telecoms as well as general trends in telecoms which affect them. If I am selling to specific end users on behalf of partners, then I could be selling into any industry type. I will try and find out a little bit about what they do and see if I can quickly source some interesting material which will be relevant. Generally speaking though, I keep it to telecoms and how communication is changing and how it affects the world they operate in.

If I am selling to a specific end user in any industry, my job is to educate them on how communications is changing, what is possible, and how it can enhance their lives and make them more money.

Many sales professionals do not sell into a specific sector or vertical market so it is impossible to do an industry fact finding mission for every pitch and meeting, but even one small thing they do not know about the world they operate in can make all the difference. Remember it is like being a parent, you do not need to know everything—just more than your child! So if this is you, then your job is to gather as much as you can about your industry and service and how its changes will impact what they do.

Often though, salespeople who sell to different industries do sell to the same audience or job role or department within a company. If this is you, then tailor your knowledge to that audience. For example, if you sell to quality control departments then find out what you can about their job type in relation to the list above. Read quality control journals and find out what you can about what is happening in their particular job function. This may sound obvious, but do you do it?

So let's say that you sell gym equipment to gyms and corporate companies from many different industries. If this is you, then maybe you could uncover these facts:

- 47% of people know someone who quits work because of stress.
- Gyms at work or access to a gym which is promoted by companies account for a reduction of 27.8% in absences from work.
- Every dollar invested in the health of an employee saves $5.50 in related costs.

These are some facts I found out with a relatively quick search. With more insight you could come up with far more interesting facts and trends than these. Using this example your job is to source as much interesting data as possible about:

- Productivity in the workplace
- Trends in fitness in companies
- The trends in different types of exercise
- What is happening to gyms generally
- What the dollar return is for every dollar invested (see above!)
- Why people join gyms, what makes them stay and how that relates to your products
- What your equipment actually does and why that type of equipment is what they need
- How are their competitors using your equipment to gain competitive advantage?

So how does this apply to you and what you do? How can you do the same, and what would make a real difference to your sales by having this type of information? Can you see yet how this would make a huge difference to your approach and your results? If not, then don't worry, as probably right now you will be thinking that this is a lot of hassle and you don't see the reward. All will become clear, I promise!

How You Are Going to Use This Information in the Real World

Depending on your audience, industry and product, the amount of interesting and useful data will vary significantly. As in most things in life, it is about balance and reading the situation in front of you to see what is appropriate. In a short while I am going to go through the process, and after that it will be a lot clearer to you how this information can be used practically.

There is no doubt about it, the majority of my time is spent discussing how I can help a client based on what is possible by using what we do as an example. I don't sit there with long presentations on interesting facts which are not relevant about wider industry trends.

As you prepare for delivering educational based sales, and as we go through the sales process, keep in mind that there are different types of information required.

Did You Know?

A lot of the time I use "did you know?" sentences. These can be used almost anywhere at any time. "Did you know?" sentences are very useful to capture someone's attention in a brief encounter where you need to make a quick impression. They are an attention seeking tool which grabs your audience, giving you credibility at the same time. In presentations I use them in batches of three. When I present I start with a "did you know?" and then a quick follow up with two "did you also know?" statements. Batches of three facts work well as that is really the maximum amount the brain can take in at any one time.

If you can, and you have the practical time, it is a good rule to aim for three responses of "I didn't know that; that is interesting and useful to know." If you do that, you have your audience—you have separated yourself from the crowed and you will be pushing against an open door from then on.

If you are in a casual situation or networking environment then probably one or two facts would suffice, as there is generally not enough time to get into that deep a conversation. As I said, you will need to read every situation and be nimble, so the key here is to have a storage of interesting RELEVANT facts, and be ready to use them when you can.

Note the relevant part. I have seen people come out with interesting facts in presentations, trying to be clever but they are not relevant to the conversation in any way. You have to be relevant on some level or otherwise your audience will switch off after the fun and interesting facts have finished. No use discussing the interesting mating patterns of pandas while pitching corporate life assurance!

Gather your interesting facts and remember them, they are very useful and can engage you very quickly with your audience.

Graphs, Charts and Trends

Graphs, charts and trend analysis should be used as a way to either deliver your "did you know" statement or as a backup to it. Nobody likes death by analysis, and unless your presentation calls for it, use these sparingly.

They need to be hard hitting, relevant, easy to see and quick to soak in. I am going to cover presentations in detail later, but for now this type of information is only useful for marketing material and presentations.

They can be fantastic tools for capturing information as a "did you know" on marketing material. A picture paints a thousand words and the visual impact can be dramatic. Your industry analysis should drag up some interesting trends which lead you to pictures you can use in hard and soft material. Do not be afraid to use other people's data (as long as you give them credit).

If you have the funds available to you, then get your own research completed and create your own proprietary data which will give you even more credibility.

Structured and Unstructured Knowledge

Up until now I have been talking about structured knowledge—information which you have at your fingertips, on a laptop and pre-prepared. Most of what you do, however, will not be structured and will not be possible to access via your laptop at the exact time you need it. Being a natural, unforced salesperson is critical to your success, so if you are diving for your tablet or computer every time you engage with a prospect then you are in trouble.

Where most professional salespeople need to spend most of their time in preparing for educating their clients is in general understanding. By that I mean general understanding of what is happening in their industry and general understanding in their product and how it applies to their audience.

The majority of my time is spent in non-structured discussions where I need to be nimble and think on my feet while being relaxed and in control. If I have to scramble around searching my brain to find information which I must know, then I am in trouble. I am always trying to appear relaxed, in control and very knowledgeable, so my audience knows instantly that I know what I am talking about. You do not have to know everything, but you do need to know more than your audience and come across as humble enough to always be learning, but knowledgeable enough to be adding value now.

By the way, do not underestimate your audience; some of them will be remarkably well informed as the information I am covering in this book is also very relevant for buyers as well as sellers. Some of them take their buying role very seriously and professionally indeed. Take time to understand your audience and their knowledge level. Often I find that sometimes when clients say they don't know much at all it is a big fat lie!

This is where your time spent reading up and educating yourself on all aspects of what you do and how it works is critical. Once you fully understand something, then you can apply its use in any given situation. If you only understand a part of what you do, then you will not be able to apply it to new situations. You will not understand how you can help someone solve a particular issue if you cannot apply your knowledge.

For example: let's say you are selling video conferencing into a large local enterprise company and they already have an ABC system installed which is only three years old. If you know that your system integrates with it, adds value in two key areas, and that your system adds a 20% higher take up rate by working with ABC system that results in a 15% reduction in travel expenses which pays for itself in two years, you have an opportunity. Instead of saying, "OK, thank you, I will call you when your system reaches its end of life," you can say, "That is great news, let me help you get the most out of what you are already doing; I can show you how to use the technology you already have to maximum effect."

When sales trainers say, "Do not take no for an answer," they are not only living in 1973, they also do not help salespeople understand how to get past it. Battering prospects with the same old crap you and your competitors have always used is not the answer. No maybe, just ignorance on the buyer's side, in which case it is your role to educate them until their no is an "informed" no and not an "ignorant" no. Sometimes no just means no; so as long as you have done your job properly and educated them, then learn to walk away, at least for a while!

It does take time to gather knowledge about what you do, as you need technical, pricing, commercial, contractual, marketing, application and support knowledge about your product or service, so there is a lot to take in. I appreciate that it is not an overnight process, but do not be lazy and rest on your previous experience. My father (who is a great salesperson by the way!) says about many people "they don't have 20 years' experience; they have one year of experience repeated 20 times!" How true this is. Most people do not take any time out to learn more, be more and do more—they just repeat what they have learned so far, done what they have always done and what others around them have always done. As we know, that is not good enough anymore, and eventually it will get you killed, from a professional point of view.

You must tool up and get skilled in fact-gathering, expand your knowledge, and you must completely understand what you are doing or you will eventually get found out and you will not be able to play at the level you need to play at in order to be the best.

Develop the skill of gathering structured information you can use in certain sales situations and also develop the skill of always helping your audience know more and more every time you interact with them. If you do not know the answer, go and find out and then learn it and teach it to them.

Competitor Analysis – Counter Intelligence

The other day I was approached by the owner of the biggest trade show in our industry and asked if I would like to do a head-to-head with one of our competitors at the show as a bit of an interactive battle in front of an audience. I obviously said yes, as this is free advertising and I get to pitch to an audience of prospects for free; no hesitation required.

The prospect of doing this got me thinking about how to approach competitor analysis, and actually what is the best way to deal with competitors in the new age of value-based selling? In this scenario my competitor will be sitting next to me on stage so I have to be as I should be: clear, concise, show integrity and be careful not to put him down in order to build myself up. What a great test!

What do you say about your competitors when you are asked or you know they are against you on a particular bid? Do you put them down or do you compare yourself to them in some way? I always try and build some level of relationship with ours, as my industry is large in terms of value, but it is small in terms of everyone knowing everyone else.

My outcome is to be the only choice left for my prospect, so actually I do not spend time focusing on what they do that we don't and what we do that they don't. If I am asked a direct question about competitors then I comment, but I never put them down and I always say that they have a good company, but that we add value in these three key areas (always use three by the way as people remember in threes). My complete assumption when I engage with prospective clients is that they are doing business with us and that there is no reason to be doing it with our competition. The reason for this fairly arrogant stance is that I know I am going to add so much value to them that they will have no choice in the end.

Very often I have to unseat our competitors from my prospect as they are already dealing with them. If I gather information about my competitors and I know their weaknesses and strengths, then I pick my value statements carefully as I want to be measured on the value we add and not against the value they already get. There must be enough of a difference for them to warrant a change to us, so I have to add as much value as possible and not win the business based on price or putting down their current provider.

So many times I have seen salespeople try to win against competitors based solely on price and as I am sure you are more than aware this is a very short term game to play. You need to study your competitors, know where you have a competitive advantage and play to your strengths, which highlight their weaknesses. For example our biggest competitor is better than us technically and far larger, so I cannot try to win on that basis. We pitch based on being easy to do business with, we go the extra mile to help, and we continually educate our clients on what is going on in the market and what we are doing to help them win more business. They are large, we are quicker.

If you are a smaller business pitching against larger ones, then you have to find a unique difference or you will get killed by a bigger, stronger army. Teaching your clients how to be better, become more efficient and how to make more money will set you apart. If you add enough value you won't need to worry about your competition but you can be sure that they will be worried about you!

Summary of What You Need to Know

The most important start you can make is to get your mind-set right. Get the mind-set of a teacher first—the mind-set of a salesperson who is there to help, guide and add value, ALWAYS.

Gather as many facts as you can from quick burst information – for use on the phone and face to face. Use trend analysis, white papers and structured information for presentations and marketing material. Be a machine in educating yourself on your industry, your product and your audience's drivers and you will be putting yourself so far ahead of your competition that you will be winning business hand over fist.

Do not stop seeking new information; keep learning and keep finding out interesting things which your audience does not know, but which will help them. Be able to hold a conversation at many levels technically, but avoid being a techie. If you sell beds, understand how they are made and what difference they make in people's lives, but you don't need to be able to make one yourself—leave that to others.

Gather as much information as you can and store it, keep it so you can access it quickly and share it with others. You will be tested a lot when you work like this and soon your colleagues will be leaning on you for help and information. It is worth the time and effort it takes to get the best information. The majority of your research time is taken up initially, but the ongoing part does not take that long. If you have the resources then get others to find the sources of information for you, but you must then take over and soak the information in yourself.

Your aim is to be an expert, someone who is seen as the go-to person, someone who gets the call from a prospect because they have a specific question not because they want to beat you up on price.

How to Get in Front of the Right People

I don't know about you, but getting through the door to even get with someone who is even vaguely interested in what you have to say is getting harder, not easier. Nobody has time anymore. People hide behind voicemail all the time and gatekeepers are getting better and better at keeping cold calls at bay.

When I started in sales I sold over the phone cold to decision makers. It was hard work, but fun. And if you were any good at it then there were great rewards; as long as you played the numbers game you would eventually get what you wanted. Today I would not like to be doing the same strategy as the market has changed so much.

So many of our resellers complain that they cannot get through the door and if they could then they would be able to win so much more business. Seeing how many of them actually make sales, I am not convinced of that, but the point remains that getting in front of the right people is getting harder and harder.

So ... how do you do it in this climate and in these increasingly busy times?

You basically have two choices: you can go where they are and get in front of them or you can capture their attention somehow long enough to get into a conversation where something happens in your favour.

Either way is good and your sales process will depend on your method of attack. I am going to cover the main ways of achieving this by adding value and using education so you can stay far ahead of the competition, which will give you a far higher success rate with more decision makers and influencers.

I am going to start with the hardest and the lowest conversion rate methods and then get to easier and higher touch solutions as I go along.

Cold Calling

As I said, I like cold calling; I find that when I get into it, it becomes enjoyable. It absolutely has its place in sales, and for many industries—especially business to consumer—it is often the primary way of getting business through the door. Cold calling is relevant when high volume is required, the sales cycle is short, and the contractual value is low.

There are so many great books and instructional DVDs on cold calling, I do not need to go through specific techniques here. If you want to get into scripting and details on how to get through gatekeepers and so forth, then read or listen to anything by Chet Holmes; he is a genius in that area.

What I am going to cover now is how to be strategic with your cold calling and how to use education to its maximum advantage. I will use specifics where relevant.

How many times have you had a cold call in the last 12 months and listened to more than five seconds of it but not less than a minute? Quite a few times, I would guess. How many of those calls were good enough to capture your attention to last long enough for them to even tell you what they did? Not many I would bet.

The problem with the vast majority of cold calling is that the script sounds like a script and the assumption is that the person on the other end of the line cares enough about your agenda. He doesn't!

You have interrupted people from what they were doing, and unless they have a compelling reason to listen to you within five seconds, you may as well put the phone down yourself and save them the bother.

Quick fire short burst interesting facts are the key here. Remember the "did you knows" from your earlier fact finding lesson? This is where they are really important and very useful. If you get two to three into the conversation quickly, then you start to build yourself up as a credible authority who knows what you're talking about.

When you are on the phone you must move away from the following: this is who I am, this is my company, this is my product, this is how I can help you save money, make money and so forth. The recipient of your call could not care less.

Instead, approach it from the following position: I know what you do, and based on my questions and experience I know what information you need to solve the pain in your life, and at the same time I can make you look good.

So let's say, for example, you sell office relocation services. Your goal is to get a rep in to see your prospect to discuss the company's office move requirements. Traditionally cold calls may have gone like this:

"Hi my name is Steve and I work for Yea de Yea, Ltd. How are you today? We specialise in office relocations and I am calling to see if you are planning an office move in the next twelve months."

If the answer is no, then it is over and even if the answer is yes your prospect will probably say no because there is no relationship, rapport or reason for them to care. If they do say yes then really all you can do from there is try and get a bit of information to help you out, book a meeting and pray they don't cancel. Basically this is an old school, numbers game-based pitch.

How about if you use education as a basis for the pitch:

Let's say that the goal is not to book a meeting so you can tell him how wonderful you are but to book a session with your company educating him on office moves, entitled "The Top Five Ways to Save a Fortune and Increase your Profits with your New Office."

Maybe the call would go something like this:

"Hi my name is Steve and I work for Yea de Yea, Ltd. We are experts in office efficiency and we provide free education on the latest office trends and advise people just like you on how to maximise every aspect of their office environment. In fact, did you know that 80% of new offices could save $100,000 if they changed their desks to round ones?" (Note: made up fact about round desks.)

After this you can then hit them with two more interesting facts which will make you an expert in their eyes. Then when you have set yourself up as an expert, ask some questions and then book in the training session either as part of a group or as a one on one.

Do you see the difference? My pitch here may not be perfect and you will probably be able to come up with a far better one for yourself, but the point here is to educate and not cajole, to impart knowledge without brow beating until they give in.

I know in telecoms many people still call prospects offering to save them money as their way in, seriously! That is so far from what is required that raising yourself above the norm is really easy in my industry.

If you change your attitude on the phone to one where you know you add value, then no amount of rejections will stop you from calling because what you have to offer is genuine and different. You will also have total believability, which is everything.

This does not just apply to cold calling on the phone, however. The same principles apply to any initial conversation. What happens if you meet someone by chance at a BBQ and you find out that he or she would be in your target audience? Maybe you sell personal finance and she is a person

...

The same principles apply, when they ask you what you do for a living. What do you say? "I sell insurance," or "I am an independent financial advisor." I hope not! How about, "I help people save a fortune," or "I teach people how to make a solid fortune which lasts for generations." You may find this too cheesy or awkward, but you get the point; tell them how you add value, not what product you sell.

Establish yourself as the expert in your field as quickly as you can in the conversation so people will come to you with relevant questions. Every industry can be made interesting to most people. Also, please do not be too stiff or rigid with it; people hate that. They like relaxed and confident people who know where they are going and can smile or even laugh at themselves along the way.

Cold calling is a great art and it still has its place in selling; however it should be treated as a profession and not as a place to start 21-year-olds who are poorly trained and who don't care about what they do. Maybe it is fine for selling windows, but not for professional services to an educated audience. With that in mind, here are some other areas of cold calling which may add value to you or your teams:

- Timing of calls – Directors are best called early in the morning or just after hours as they are around and gatekeepers are often not there.
- Do what you say you are going to do – If you agree to call someone back in two weeks, be professional and call them in two weeks, not before.

- Thank them for their time – please do **not** do this, it puts them in control and puts you down. Appreciate their attention and say "good to talk to you" or something like that, but NEVER thank them for their time.
- Dates – when booking a meeting only offer two dates, and be specific. It is like asking someone what colour they like, you only ask them if they like blue or green; that is their choice.
- Follow up – Every time you speak to someone about anything, before you complete the sale create a reason to email him. It keeps you in his inbox and in his mind.
- Constant education – when you find out something interesting which is relevant to your audience send a personal email saying "Hi, I found this interesting article / piece of information and thought you would like it …" This keeps you in the customer's mind and reinforces your position as an authority.
- Research who they are – I am constantly amazed by the amount of salespeople who do not even look at their prospect's website or social media output. There will be so many clues about how you can add value to them from this basic, publically available information. You can also mention what you have found on the call, making you look like you have researched the company, and you have a genuine interest in what they are doing.
- Not all prospects are equal – it is always worth making a list of targeted prospects to work on rather than a general list of everyone. This allows you to specialise, focus and research who would be your best clients. There are whole books written on this

one subject so take time to focus. I have rejected prospective clients after I have spoken to them as they are not clients who I can help the most. Perhaps pick a particular vertical for a few weeks and specialise on that vertical. The more you practice with a specific audience the better you get.

The key to cold calling when using education is to get a very interesting relevant fact in quickly so they think to themselves, "No, I didn't know that; it is interesting. OK, I will give this person a few more minutes." Once you have captured their attention you need to establish your credibility very quickly so they believe that you know what you are talking about. Prove your knowledge and experience, make sure you come from a source of helping others just like them. You are not showing off, you are linking their issues with others like them whom you have been able to successfully help.

Once you have caught their attention and proven your credibility, it is now time to move the conversation on to the next stage. I suggest a training session of some description. If your goal is to set a meeting, then book it as a training session instead of a sales pitch. Even better if you actually have arranged a local training session for people like them so you can be time efficient, getting many prospects in one room. I remember when I ran a web company, we specialised in social media for business and I laid on a one hour session at the local university (always a good place to offer education), so we could educate people on how social media was affecting business. Over 80 people turned up and I remember that number well as only 60 had said they were coming. How often does that happen!

I invited two other local people who I knew had specific expertise and we all presented, education only, no sales pitch apart from a "one minute shameless self-promotion" bit at the end. It worked brilliantly and we used it in a lot of marketing and promotional material as well to extend the tail of its effectiveness.

It is always easier to cold call with an invitation to something free than try to get them interested in a pitch, or book an appointment for a rep who "is in their area next week." Also, for the ones who do not turn up, you now have a reason to go and see them separately. Only last week we provided a free training session and several people dropped out. Since then I have easily booked meetings with four of them and one was signed up a few days ago. I would never have gotten in to see them if we had not offered the education session first.

So in summary, effective cold calling must contain these three elements:

1. Grab their attention with hard hitting relevant facts;
2. Keep their attention by raising your credibility;
3. Move them to the next stage by offering to educate them for their own benefit, for free.

Your words and detail about how you do this will depend on your industry and your audience, so common sense is of course required, but the strategy should be the same.

Marketing Material

This is not a marketing book so this will be brief.

It is critical that the rest of the sales collateral and marketing material reflects the educational and credibility sales process. For example, tender responses and proposals are, just like traditional sales calls, the wrong way around. They often follow the same pattern of this is who we are, this is what we do, this is our price, these are some of our clients, the end. How dull!

You have to stand out in all your marketing, and using your educational approach is key to doing this. I write many articles and press releases as I want them to be from our sales department, not our marketing department. When I do, I always talk about the fact that we educate our partner base constantly and I always try to actually teach something as part of the article. Recently I signed up a significant partner for us because in an article I said that now you can get Chinese landline numbers outside China. We had never done it and actually as I write, we still have not, but the MD of that company saw what I had written and it interested him and so he called us.

When we met I asked him if he knew who we were before he rang and he did but he had no reason to work with us, or so he believed. If we had not educated him, he still would not have a reason to call us.

We won a national award this year which was voted for by a panel of experts from our industry. When we won I asked one of the panel why we won and he said that the main reasons were our growth, our education program and ethos. Imagine how much marketing we got out of that!

Make sure all your marketing material follows this same process. Use the material you gathered from your research to show off what you know and what is happening. You can use "did you knows" in your printed material as well.

Use specifics in what you write. Numbers are great and they have impact. Pictures which demonstrate your point are even better, and graphs are also very useful. It is far better to say that 75% of people who have back surgery do not need to, than we help people with back pain.

So use your research, be specific, build your credibility and talk about how you teach your prospects and clients. Make sure your paper, web and other marketing material is aligned with your sales message. Step away from all the usual, same-as-everyone-else marketing collateral; be different and show that you add value all the time.

Partnering – the 21st Century Way of Selling

As it has become so much harder to grab the attention of the best prospects, many organisations are now turning to partnerships to get them into the right places and in front of the right people. If you are a technology led company with relatively poor sales and commercial teams, then this may well be the way for you to get more business through the door. Having said that, many of the best sales companies in the world also use partnerships to gain a competitive advantage.

Up until now I have very much concentrated on separating you and your competition through education, and that, of course, is a huge part of this book, but so is the need for leverage through strategic relationships. If you are going to thrive in any economy and in the new world order, you need to look at working with others as much as you can.

I love building businesses which work through partners. Mostly because you get access to their client base without the cost of acquisition, but also because they can bring so many new ideas and opportunities that are not available with direct selling only. As I said, we only sell through partners in our business and we live and die by the service we give to them. Partnering is very much a 21st century way of selling; the leverage and the speed to market are beyond compare. Apple, Microsoft, Cisco, Dell and a multitude of other large and small brands use partnerships to sell and distribute their products and services. Do you? They may call them franchises or VAR's or channel partners or a multitude of other names, but they are still using partnerships.

Many companies and old school sales professionals believe that partnerships are not as effective. They believe they lose control over the client, the sales process, the relationship, and they believe they have to give too much margin away. Sometimes this may be true, but mostly because organisations do not know how to build an effective partnership proposition.

There are many types of partnership formats you can use to get in front of your target audience:

Direct Partners

Direct partners are partners you sell through directly; they rely on you for their income and you are a source for a core product or service of theirs, which they take to their market. You contract with them and they sell to the end user. Generally this is not an exclusive arrangement, otherwise that would be more of a distribution model. Direct partners are often called channel partners.

Generally they come in two types: resellers and dealers / agents. You may call them different names but resellers mark up your service and sell on in their name, and dealers sell your product or service with your badge on it and often with your contract of sale. Retailers would be resellers and affiliates would be dealers, for example.

In our industry many organisations are dealers, as the deeper the technology the harder it is to provide support, billing and the right contract fulfilment. Becoming a dealer where all you have to do is sales is very attractive to many companies. In fact, my main business in my thirties was a dealership which I eventually sold, but only after years of great cash flow and a fairly stress-free business life.

Resellers tend to be larger partners as they require the expertise internally to bill, sell and provide support to the client base. Because of this they will get better terms and should be providing larger volumes.

If you are looking at setting up partnership arrangements as part of your future business strategy, then make sure you can look after the most appropriate types of partners for your industry or product. Cast your net wide at first if you are unsure and eventually the market will tell you what types of partnership it wants.

Strategic/ Distribution Partners

These partners often have some exclusivity, either over price or territory. They distribute your product or service and they may well have direct partners of their own. A wholesaler would be a good example in the traditional retail world. A lower margin is expected here, but higher transaction frequency or volume is the key to making it work. Also, it is lower touch from your point of view in terms of the end user. Most of the time you would never meet their partners or end clients as the margins and process of sale do not allow it.

Introducers

Introducers are partners who basically pass you to their clients or their clients to you. A doctor's surgery passing rehabilitation clients to a chiropractor would be a good example of this type of relationship.

Introducers are often the lowest cost financially as they do the least amount of work. Sometimes they do not want or cannot take any commission or income for passing you leads or direct clients, especially in medical circumstances. Because of this they can be very profitable indeed.

You get to control the client relationship in this arrangement and you get to contract with the end user so you can cross sell later, if appropriate.

White Label Partners

White label partners are ones which either take your product or service—with all of the relevant sales material, processes, methodology and digital marketing, and label it as their own. Often seen as a web based model (but doesn't have to be), white labelling is very effective when you have a nailed-on sales process and excellent material.

Your partners essentially acts as a franchisee in many respects, but with their own brand. You are the back engine and order fulfilment agent. In this arrangement, it is impossible to get in front of the end user and influence the sales process; you can only generally speak to the partners, but not through them.

For white labelled partnerships you need professionals who know how to work with partners and get the best out of them. You also need excellent contracts, as the cost to set up this type of relationship is often much higher for you. They must also be the right type of partners, and you should spend time making sure they are the one. For example, if you develop a white label tool for companies to run holiday home rentals, you will need to find the right type of company with relevant experience who can deliver or pay a lot up front; otherwise you will incur a lot of set up costs on your own.

Joint Venture

A joint venture is a much tighter, more legally binding arrangement, where essentially you partner with a company to sell yours and/or their products where you share risk, capital and reward. Joint ventures are common when entering into new markets or where launching a product or service is far too expensive for one organisation, like film making, for example.

Joint ventures can be project based, and be specific relating to a market, area or timescale. As with all partnerships though, joint ventures require significant legal input and advice before you go down this path.

JV's can be very powerful if they work. As the old saying goes, "One horse can pull one tonne, but two can pull over 20." However, as they are so inextricably linked to another party, the other party must be the right one or the whole venture will be a disaster.

Strategic Alignment

Synergy is the key here. Strategic alignment is where you partner with someone or a company because you complement each other. Perhaps you sell to the same audience or the same industries and so you can share contacts and sales opportunities.

You can use any of the above types of partnerships in order to make the commercials work, but the key is that you find a way that works for you both.

For example, you may sell industrial kitchens into hotels and you may partner with a law firm that works in that industry as they look after the contracts for people buying or renovating hotels. You may also partner with a fit out company that renovates hotels, or you may partner with a catering company that already works with all the hotels in an area. The amount of companies with which you may work with are often far more than you think—just think big and see who is interested.

Many times there is no commercial agreement or commission paid here, as it can be a reciprocal arrangement where you keep an eye out for each other. Over time, these relationships can flourish and become more established partnerships. You can often try them out on a handshake and see how it goes.

Network Marketing

For many products, network marketing (multi-level marketing) has been an extremely effective way to market. If you don't know what network marketing is, then have a look on the web. Basically it is the distribution of products and services through a personal network of people. It is not to be confused with pyramid selling.

Network marketing, if done right, can be extremely successful, and some companies become multibillion dollar organisations by using this form of distribution arrangement.

It works very well for FMCG and high margin repeat purchase items like soap, and travel and nutrition based products. Some of the biggest examples are:

- Amway
- Forever Living
- Herbalife
- Legal Shield

If you have a new product to bring to the market, and you think it may fit this partnership model, then this may well be the way forward for you. You will defiantly need an expert to help you set it up as there is a lot of hard work involved, but once it is set up then you can really make a fortune if the product and the model are excellent.

So what was the point of taking you through all the different type of partnerships available to you? Many reasons, actually.

- You may already sell in this way, in which case there could be a type of partnership you had not thought of in the past which could work for you.
- You may only sell direct, and so maybe partnering could be the way forward for you to get more sales and more brand awareness.

- You may be looking to enter into new territories, and so partnerships may be the only way to get a foothold there. Barriers such as language, local clients or just sheer distance can be removed.

I have seen so many businesses that work as an island, and get frustrated with how sales are going, not realising that using only one of the above arrangements would make a massive impact on their profitability.

In the 21st century, folding your arms and saying *it's all mine* will not work. Collaboration is critical to success, and if you and your business are to thrive then you must look outside your walls to see who is out there; see who can help you sell more and make more money.

In order for partnerships to work effectively for you, you must add value or have some type of intellectual property (IP). The more value you add which is yours alone, the stronger the relationships you can forge. IP can be provided in many forms but can be distinguished, for example, as:

- Technology patents
- Territory exclusivity
- Exclusive access to methodologies or technology
- Experience
- Distribution process
- Outstanding service levels
- Price
- Lower barrier to entry
- Deployment experience

- Better education

There are many more. The point here is that many companies think they cannot get the right partnerships because they sell the same products and services as many other companies. However, as the list above shows, there are many ways to separate yourself from the crowd. Partners often just need one of them as a reason to do business with you.

Also, many of your best partnership companies may simply have never before been approached or have an existing relationship which is not working.

Recently I approached a company that provides fit outs to large companies. Basically when a company wants to move or upgrade its offices, it does the construction, the relocation, the furniture and so on. The pitch was that we would provide the telecoms for its companies, as when they move they always need some kind of telecoms help. Interestingly, they used to use a one-man-band consultant for this, but he got greedy and did not provide the right level of service to their clients, so they terminated the relationship with him and signed with us.

We offered to add more value and work closely with them and their fit out teams to provide a single point of contact for the customer, with an educational approach as described earlier. They had also realised that they needed someone like us as they were being left behind with advancing technology, and they did not offer any assistance on this subject, which left them vulnerable.

Interestingly, they did not want any commission from us and we were allowed to contract directly with the end customer. We added significant value and assistance to their customer base, which meant they could secure more business. What a great way to get in with the right people at the right time, and to top it off, be introduced by a trusted advisor who already has the attention of all the key decision makers.

What partnerships can you work on that could develop the same level of sales opportunities for you?

The Greatest One-to-One Way to the Right Contact

Over the last 2,000 years plus, the best way to sell to anyone was to gain his trust and make him feel comfortable with you and what you had to say. Nothing in this regard has changed. People still buy in the same way; human nature has not altered. What has altered are the most effective ways to get them to this place. I have already covered many ways to do this, from partnerships to effective cold calling, but by far the most effective method on a one-to-one direct selling basis is networking.

Looking back, most of the largest opportunities in my life have started because I met someone in a networking situation. I network everywhere, from nights out to rounds of golf to specific networking events. I love it and I am really good at it primarily because I enjoy it and I am not afraid to maximise its potential.

The reason I love it is because I can be me; I am selling in a comfortable, relaxed way and I can create rapport so much easier in a relaxed environment than over the phone or in structured meetings.

How would you be if I put you in a room with the top 100 prospects you have? Would you be able to effectively network the room and maximise the opportunity, or would you shrivel up and stand in the corner alone?

Effective networking can put you right in the face of the person you need to influence to get a deal. If you sell to board level people and struggle with getting to see them, then in my experience networking is best way to do it. If your business suits all business people in general, or business owners, then networking is absolutely critical for you.

Effective networking takes practice and time. I remember when I first went to a structured networking event in my home town years ago. I did not know what to say or do. I was tongue tied and flustered whenever I spoke to someone. People would ask me what I did and I could not concisely tell them at all.

As time progressed I developed a short, concise, educationally informative and flexible pitch so people could very quickly grasp what I did and how it might be able to add value to them. If it could not, then fine, but at least it saved me time and it was very efficient.

Networking can be very efficient, but you have to be focused. If you go to your local networking events you will find many small businesses and one man armies trying desperately to sell to you, so be careful. If your target audience is multinationals, then a local small town gathering is unlikely to contain the people you need to speak to. HOWEVER, you never know who they know, and many, many times I have been referred by people I have met who knew someone who needed what I did.

There are basically two types of networking - structured and unstructured.

Structured Networking

Structured networking is generally an event that has networking in the title—simple. These events range from speed networking to full blown industry-specific events with key decision makers in the room. I know companies that have spent in excess of $40,000 to be at a networking event which had pre-arranged meetings with the right people. Their view was that all they had to do was close one deal and it was worth the price of the event. In our industry, for example, there is an annual event which costs a supplier in excess of $25,000 for three days and two nights. All the top resellers attend for free to be pitched to by companies like ours. There are structured meetings during the day which are great, but often the best contacts are made in the bar afterwards.

In my experience speed networking – a bit like speed dating without the fun – is too much noise with people just handing out as many business cards as they can to each other. Nobody really listens to the other, and when you are finished it is really hard to remember anything anyone said. Generally speaking, the more intimate and longer time you have with specific individuals, the better. Lunches are good and breakfasts are great as they don't eat too much into your day.

At structured networking events, people know why they are there, which is to sell. The issue with that is that they don't all have their agenda, and they are so hell bent on selling that they are often not buying. Also the room is full of salespeople and if they are very senior then the company may be too small for you. I know many people who are very successful at these events, and I will cover later how they do it.

If you are offering products or services that target individuals, for example law firms, medical services, nutrition etc., then this can work very well for you. If you are selling oil tankers, then unless the room is likely to have the purchasing director of an oil company in it, you will probably be wasting your time.

Also, the vast majority of businesses at organised networking events are quite small and in my experience, there is an oversupply of lawyers and accountants. So if you are selling to lawyers and accountants, then this really will be for you.

Sometimes – especially in larger cities – there are networking events which are more exclusive, and I often used to go to one near me which was for director level and above only of companies that had a certain turnover and employee size. This was great, and a very different atmosphere from the throw-as-many-cards-out-as-you-can over a pizza networking evening.

Efficiency of time in sales is critical, and you can waste many, many hours of untargeted networking if you are not careful. If you are looking for events, then start by trying the commitment-free ones. You will probably get charged for drinks, lunch and so forth, but you need to be able to try it out before you commit to any long term agreement to attend. Some are weekly and demand that you attend a certain number of times, which is fair enough if you get regular business from it, but a real bind if you don't.

Start with local chambers of commerce or general business organisations to see what is out there. Better still, find one which contains the audience you sell to. For example, if you sell financial software then attend the accountants networking group (if they will let you in) or the local finance directors' forum – I doubt it will be that easy, but you never know. Failing that, if there is one you do not qualify to attend, then offer to speak for free and show them that you are an expert. Use the educational information we covered earlier and add value to their short time with you.

Generally speaking, the more consultative and niche-y the product you are selling, the more targeted you need to be with the group you attend. There will definitely be a group somewhere which suits you, and one which contains a lot of the right people for you to get to know. Look hard and check it out as it can be very efficient and effective for you.

Unstructured Networking

I am networking all the time. I take as many opportunities as I can to meet the right people. I find it far easier to create a meaningful relationship with a prospect over a dinner or round of golf or at a sports event than over the phone or at a structured networking event.

Unstructured networking events are those events where people are there, but for another reason apart from pitching or be pitched to. Examples are industry dinners, professional events, golf days, product launches and so forth. Your industry will have its own set of these and your target audience its own as well, so do take time to get to know them and be there.

Unstructured events are efficient, as generally everyone is more relaxed and much more approachable. It is often easier to have a longer conversation if it is going well, and easier to walk away if it is not.

Let me give you a great example which highlights exactly why I network in this way all the time. While I was writing this section of the book, I got a message to connect with someone on LinkedIn whom I met a couple of nights ago at an industry awards dinner. He is the Managing Director of a large telecoms company who, to be honest, I had not really heard of. We were sitting next to each other for the dinner and we got on very well. The only business we discussed was the "what do you do" conversation, which lasted about three to four minutes. After that we just had fun and relaxed.

I gave him my card and he did not give me his for whatever reason. But today he connected to me on LinkedIn and a couple of messages later he suggested I speak to his co-director to pitch our product as they are currently looking for a supplier of what we do. Now there is no way in the world that I would ever have gotten that introduction normally as I did not know what his company was and have not come across it before. If I had rung him up and cold called, then I doubt it would have gone that far, and if it did then it would have taken quite a while to get to this point – a very warm introduction to the right person from his boss!

I have no doubt you have done this yourself many times, but often as professional salespeople we forget to get ourselves out of our normal selling routine and get amongst it in other ways.

I also love corporate events and any business social event I can get to which contains my potential audience, as the networking is great and it is fun. I know a lot of salespeople who ignore many events they should be at because they feel uncomfortable. If you feel like this, then you really do need to get over it and get good at networking wherever you are. The world has changed, and traditional methods of getting in front of the right people have evaporated. Networking has become more critical to sales success, and you need to be outstanding at it.

If I had a choice, I would put unstructured networking above structured as a priority, as personally my success percentage is higher and the people often are of a better quality. Awards dinners, trade shows and business social events often have higher management levels and more decision makers at them, so they are very effective if you are selling into a corporate environment. If you are selling to all individuals, then all types of networking will be great for you.

How to Network Like a Pro

Networking is an art form, and it is certainly something which takes time and effort to become effective at. There is absolutely a right and wrong way to network, and even if you are a seasoned networker, this section will be useful in reminding you of the more subtle points that work.

The main principle in your head when you approach it should be, "I am here to be flexible and see what happens," and "I am here to connect with a couple of people to see if I can add value to anyone's life."

If you are too intense and you try too hard, it will appear unnatural and forced, and you will scare people away. This may seem obvious, but even the best can be like this and I have seen it myself too many times. All you want to say to them is, "Relax for crying out loud, you are making us all tense!" So check in with yourself as often as you can and be self-critical. Think relaxed and focused at the same time.

Smile and look happy, please. Nothing puts someone off more than a miserable sod standing in the corner being grumpy. You will have a very unsuccessful and lonely event if you are like this at all. However, please also do not be too over-the-top and fake. I remember a woman whom I used to see at many events, whom everyone would avoid because she was really trying too hard. She never got any business out of it as far as I was aware, and certainly nothing substantial and long lasting.

Take the pressure off yourself with the mind-set I outlined above. If you put pressure on yourself to walk away with ten great contacts in an hour, the chances are that you won't, and you will be setting yourself up as desperate and will appear unapproachable.

IT TAKES TIME to get good at this, and it defiantly takes time if you are going to the same regular networking events. You need to get your face known for trust to be gained and who you represent. If you have decided to go to an organised monthly or weekly meeting, then I would recommend spending the first few just getting to know the room and who the players and leaders are before going in too strong. Listen a lot to how people pitch, and watch how the good ones work the room. Some people are fantastic at this and they get a lot of business from these situations, so find them and study their approach and duplicate it.

In unstructured and one off events, you will need to seize the opportunity as you probably will not meet again and generally you will make fewer contacts, so the quality needs to be high to make it worth your while. You still must be relaxed and focused, though.

Posture is key in all situations and by this I mean you are the one holding the golden egg; you are the one with the great story to tell and the one in the room who can make a difference to some people's lives or careers, so act as such. This is the attitude you need to have when you work the room: not too cocky but have an air of "I know what I have and you will love to hear what I have to say." Sometimes you also need to take it away (in every sales situation by the way) from a prospect if she looks like she is messing you around or not taking you seriously. Over the years I have seen so many people almost apologise for what they do, look at the floor and mumble because they do not believe in what they do or in what they are selling. You don't need me to tell you how bad this is, do you?

I can see a confident, self-assured person in a networking room from a mile away, it is so rare. They shine out like a beacon for all to approach and attract. You must be this person and have this attitude; if you do, then you will win and win big, as you will rise above the masses very quickly.

This brings me on to dressing at networking events. Obviously you need to be appropriate so I am really talking about specific business based networking events here, not a round of golf. But the amount of times I have seen men and women dress unprofessionally at these events is astonishing. It is fashionable to not wear a tie these days, and sometimes I don't, but if it is a formal business event, I wear a tie and often a three piece suit as my view is I would rather be the best dressed person in the room than average. I get comments all the time on what I wear, and it not only makes me feel good, it works. I get more business because people think I am more professional and have a higher standard than others because of the way I dress. So be as smart as you can for the circumstances, and look the part. However, if you work in the software industry, for example, and turn up like that you will make a fool of yourself, so have common sense and wear the best jeans in the room!

Getting someone's business card is not a definition of success of effective networking. Getting people's business cards is easy; they can't wait to give them to you. The definition of success from networking is making more sales. I have a system where I put the cards of people I want to speak to again in my right pocket and the ones I don't in my left, so when I get back to the office one pocket full can be filed in the cylinder next to my desk!

You also do not have to hand your card out to everyone, and if you think there is no value in a certain connection then don't bother, especially if you believe you will end up on an annoying mailing list. However, do bring them, as so many times I have met people who have forgotten them, especially at unstructured events where it might not be obvious to bring them with you.

On the subject of business cards while I am here, please spend good money on their design and feel (if you are in control or can influence that purchasing) that standing out is the name of the game here, and this is one of the easy ways you can. One of our channel partners has a see-though card which is really well done, looks great and people always comment on it. Sometimes it is better to be different, and this is well worth the investment.

When I get people's cards I always use the Japanese approach and pay reverence to the card. I study it and I spend a good few seconds looking at it so people know I am taking more interest in them than everyone else does. This works very well and actually reading someone's card can sometimes reveal interesting things about them or their company. I respect every card I get regardless of who the person it and what she does, as first, you want to have a good reputation and second, you do not know who they know.

One of the main benefits of networking is the wider network of second line contacts of people in the room. One of the biggest deals I have ever done happened because of someone I met at a networking event who knew someone who could help me and also knew how right they were. I never would have met him if I had not met the first contact and shown interest in her.

If you want to be an outstanding networker, then one of your roles is to pull people together who have no benefit to you, but who have benefit to each other. If you see an obvious fit for someone, then make it happen; it is very rewarding personally, and you can be sure they won't forget you. Put people in touch and facilitate introductions as much as you can, as what goes around definitely comes around. It only takes a few minutes.

So What Do the Pros Do to Get More Sales?

A lot of effective networking is common sense, but there are some very useful rules to follow which work.

The first thing you need to do is know who you want and have targets in mind. Unless everyone in the room is a potential customer for you, then you will need to act in a targeted manner. Know your audience and if you have a finite time, be ruthless and specific.

You do need to get to your audience as quickly as possible as this is not a social event, it is a business event. If it is a social event then fine, but still if it is in business time and circumstances, then the same rules apply. I have often seen people talking to the same people month in month out—people they already know and will never do business with because it makes them feel comfortable. This is not effective and should be avoided. If you like them, invite them out for a drink later, but there is business to be done and you should be there to do it. Get out amongst it and meet as many NEW people as you can.

As I said earlier, your time management in sales is absolutely critical, as professionals we need to be the most efficient we can with as little waste in our day as possible. Networking can be a colossal waste of your time if it is not targeted at the right audience and you do not speak to the right people when they are in the room.

Often at structured networking events you may be asked to pitch to the whole room. A great local networking group which I used to attend always had "just a minute" presentations where the facilitator of the event would randomly call on people to pitch for a minute. You really needed to be ready with your pitch, as the next person could easily have been you! Make sure you have a great one minute pitch on hand for a presentation at all times, and use the education work I covered earlier to make it interesting and engaging.

When you do speak to people individually and they ask you what you do, you should follow these rules:

- Be engaging, don't be too pitchy.
- Be concise and brief (less than 30 seconds).
- Be funny if you can, people love people who are funny.
- Give an example of how you have helped people like them recently.

- As before, be educational and use your "did you knows" when talking to them.
- Qualify them in or out with well pointed questions.
- If you want to talk to them further, don't oversell; get their card and arrange a specific time to call them within the next 48 hours.
- Also ask them more interesting questions than "what do you do for a living?" Everyone asks that and it gets very dull indeed. The answer to that question will come out when appropriate.

So many times I got stuck in what seemed like endless conversations with the world's most boring people (in fact the more boring the longer it seemed to go on) and I politely listened and nodded at the appropriate times and smiled. This was very frustrating, and I distinctly remember watching the people I really wanted to see across the room leaving. I had missed the chance to speak to them; not good. Don't let this happen to you. Sometimes you do need to be ruthless (and nice at the same time). Create an excuse to leave when you have to move on.

One of the key areas to networking where people are least effective is following up. As I said earlier, you do need to create a specific time to follow up with people you want to engage with. Just saying "I'll call you soon" is not very effective. Saying "I will make sure I call you tomorrow, what time is good?" is obviously much more effective. When you do arrange a time, then stick to it, do not be late.

Every time I get a card I want and I have not managed to arrange a specific reason or time to follow up, I always send an email as soon as possible reminding them of our conversation, and if appropriate, a next step of contact. Do not leave it more than a couple of days or it will get stale and momentum will be lost. Also, if I can I try to get a personal connection in the conversation and then refer to it in the email, for example: "I hope Jonnie has a great match tomorrow," or "Enjoy your wedding anniversary," people buy people, and networking allows this level of personal connection, which traditional sales does not initially, so use it to connect with your audience.

Of course, less formal networking needs to be toned down a bit but the same process applies— engage, gain interest, be engaging, swap details, follow up, close the deal. In my experience, I will get better, more lasting relationships in more social environments, as I have more time to create a relationship and gain rapport, which in my mind is the single most important thing I can do in outstanding sales.

On the subject of less formal networking, these events often involve alcohol. At the risk of sounding like your parents, under no circumstances should you ever get yourself into an unprofessional or compromising position when there are people around who could potentially be clients or influencers who will judge you.

I love having fun and having a drink, but I always remain more sober than the average of the room I'm in, and I never have so much to drink as to compromise my professional integrity or embarrass myself or my business. The amount of chances to do so in my industry are enormous, and I have seen so many people lose respect because of what they have done with a bottle of champagne inside them. Do not let this be you; be the one who has a great time and is very sociable, but also the one who never takes it too far and always has respect for your actions, as actions always have consequences. If you feel the need to let go once and a while, do it with your friends.

Whatever type of networking works for you, make sure it results in sales which you measure so you can see how effective you are. Do not lose sight of why you are there and what your purpose is. It may be a softer sales process, but the numbers still count! In our CRM system, I have networking as a category for the source of a lead.

If after a while networking is not working for you, then instead of blaming networking, blame yourself. If your audience has been in the room, then it is your fault. If it is not in the room, then have you focused on the right events for you? If it is not working, then change your approach or the types of events you go to. Look at your pitch, how you interact with others, and how you follow up with people you have met. What questions are you asking and have you struck the right balance of focus and being relaxed? It may be worth speaking to the people who run the events you go to, as in my experience, they know everyone there and they may be able to facilitate an introduction or two to get you started.

If it really is not working for you because the people you need to speak to do not go to networking events, then maybe it is time to create your own. I know companies that have set up cocktail evenings with engaging speakers for their audience, one of which happens to be financial institutions. They invite all of their prospects and potential prospects and they make it compelling to attend, as they sell it as an informative and high-end collection of their clients' peers. It took a while to gain momentum and it costs money, but it is now very successful and they get a lot of business from it.

If you do create your own event, then certainly initially the costs will be yours to front, however, if it becomes very successful, then you may be able to charge for admission. If you do go down this road, be careful to not make it look like a pitch fest from you. Your company should act as the facilitator, and is there to get people in the room and create the environment they most want. Ask them what their industry is lacking in this regard and I am sure they will tell you. Relevant speakers who can help them is a great way to start.

My old accountants do this. They have a monthly finance form where they bring in interesting speakers and it is very well attended; they even charge for it now. It does get them a lot of new and repeat business, and it keeps their brand out there.

Also remember that if the costs are too high, find a company who also sells to your audience and partner with it to joint host the event.

So as you can see, in the 21st century some things have not really changed that much. You still have to get in the face of your audience, you still need to create rapport and relationships, and you still need to possess all the skills you always had in sales. The main difference, however, is the methods you need to employ in engaging with people and how to get in front of their faces in the first place.

Networking is a key component of this evolutionary story, and if you are not creating sales from it, then maybe now is the time. Get out there and see what you can find. If you cannot find anything which works for you, then create your own and always add as much value as possible.

Your Digital Footprint

Let's face it, in the 21st century if you do not have an online presence of some description, then you will suffer. Most salespeople do not leverage the online tools available to them enough, and therefore they miss so many opportunities to sell more.

There is no point in talking here about a website or digital marketing as there are hundreds of books and sites dedicated to maximising these resources. Also, you may work for a large organisation and so will probably have no influence on these activities anyway. What I am talking about here is your personal professional online brand. Your digital footprint.

A few years ago I ran a web marketing company helping organisations and individuals understand and maximise social media and the digital world in general to help their sales. What was astonishing to me was the lack of basic understanding in the concepts of what the web can do for traditional sales. Many companies and successful individuals I met could not see beyond their need to put up a basic and often very expensive and poorly developed website. They had little or no clue on how to create a personal brand and how to use simple online tools to get more sales.

There are two main ways to develop sales online. The first is to digitally market so you attract people to you, your company or your product. The second is to reach out through the web to connect with others so you can tell them what you do. Essentially, push and pull.

What most do is push—they set up a website and pray for people to come to them. They may even do a bit of Search Engine Optimisation (SEO) and they may pay for some ads on Google to generate some interest. All of this is relevant, but for professional salespeople like us, it is not enough.

We need to go to our audience digitally just as I have been talking about physically. All the same principles apply to the online world as they do to the physical. You still need to have integrity, understand your product, market and audience, and you still need to create rapport.

Many people are afraid of the web and social media because they don't understand them. Beyond the technology, there is nothing new to understand. If you are a great salesperson on the phone and face to face, then you will be the same online; all you have to do is act the same way and understand how to use the technology. Do not get hung up on the technology though, as once you get used to it, it is straightforward. Remember the web was created by geeks and techies who like to mystify it so they can feel important and remain above us mere mortals. What I will cover here is fairly simple to do and does not require a degree in IT.

Your Personal Brand

If you think that clients, employers and people of influence alike in your profession don't search for you online, then I'm afraid to say you are mistaken. They do!

Your online brand as a professional salesperson may sound like one of those media agency ideas where they charge you a fortune for a lot of froth and no substance, but it is not. How your company markets your product or service is one thing; how you market yourself is quite another.

The concept of a personal brand online is critical for a professional salesperson for many reasons. In your current role it will help you get more sales, and as your career develops, it can help you get better sales roles. If you own your own business, then you can replace the latter with new partners and opportunities.

Have you searched for yourself online recently? What comes up? Does anything embarrassing appear when your name is searched? Remember what goes on the web stays on the web and if you post something, it will remain on there forever (often even if you delete it). Have a search now and see what appears. Look under normal web search and images. When you are searching, remember to look past page one of the search results, as that may be where the less flattering information is found.

After your search, you may need to delete some things you don't like or have them removed from certain sites. As I said, it is often difficult or impossible to have information removed from the web, so you may have to just live with it, learn from it and move on.

Employers, prospects, clients and others now see a blurring of the lines between your professional online profile and your personal one. I have heard many stories of people looking to offer someone a job, but after an online search they found personal images they did not like (maybe one too many parties) and that was the end of that.

I am very careful about what I personally put on the web. I use Facebook for example but I am really strict about what I put up and very strict with the security settings I have on there. Only personal contacts can see anything I post or put up. I do not invite clients or professional contacts generally to connect with me personally.

If others post things about me though, I cannot control that and this may become an issue. If you see something you don't like that was posted by someone else, then ask them to take it down. Also, you should often check the security settings on your personal social media sites, as they change frequently.

So how do you manage your online brand effectively? Here are a few key principles which will guide you well:

- Make sure your LinkedIn profile is maximised (much more about this later).
- Never say anything online which is written out of anger, spite or showing off. If you need to take 10 deep breaths before posting something, then do so.

- Never react to anyone online while in the above negative states if they post something you don't like. Do stick up for yourself, but do not get involved in a fight online.
- Never belittle or denigrate someone else.
- Never post while drunk!
- Take time to understand your sharing settings on all social media platforms. It is your responsibility to make sure you know who can see what and when.
- Remember, what gets put online stays online and it is almost impossible to delete it.
- Make sure the professional pictures of you are professional.

As I said, the web is the same as the physical world in many respects; all of the human principles and traits you need to be successful offline are the same online. If you add value, you win more business, if you educate, you will win more business, and if you create quality relationships then you will win more business.

So be very conscious of your personal professional brand online and make sure that people see what you want them to see. Be professional at all times and act like you would if everyone was watching, because they may well be.

How to Sell Effectively Online

As I said, I am not going to talk about web marketing, but what I will cover is how you can engage with your audience effectively by using some simple tools.

LinkedIn (Facebook for Professionals)

LinkedIn has been called "Facebook for people with jobs" and in some respects that may be true. LinkedIn is probably the single biggest resource available to you in social media for professional, person to person sales.

If you do not have an account, then before you read any more words here go to www.linkedin.com and get one.

Once you have an account there are a few key technical parts you need to get right.

1. Make sure you have a really good professional looking picture on there. Pay for one if you need to.
2. Make sure your profile is 100% complete as you will be found more often if it is.
3. List all your main skills so people can endorse you.
4. Get at least three professional recommendations from people who have good things to say about you, preferably from clients and definitely not from your Mum!
5. On your security settings, do not allow others to see your contacts if they are not connected to you, and it is also wise to not allow anyone else to see your contacts, as in sales this is your online database.
6. Do not connect to people you do not know. Build a quality list of contacts, not a list of random people.
7. DO NOT SELL OVERTLY; contribute and add value.

There are many ways to use LinkedIn to create great contacts and make sales. Here are some I use which may help you:

Finding specific contacts you want:

The larger your network the better for many reasons, not least of which is that it is often not necessarily the people you know but the people *they* know who you can help you. If you have a network of say 50 connections, then they may know between them 5000, but if you have a connected list of 500 yourself, then they may know 50,000.

So let's say that you are looking to sell your product into Dell Corporation and you don't know anyone there. You can look on LinkedIn and see if any of your contacts do. If they do, then you can ask them to make a LinkedIn introduction, much the same as you would at a networking event. I have used this a few times to great effect, and I know people who have won large contracts because of this approach alone.

Use groups to maximum effect:

On LinkedIn there are groups for everything. You can join groups and participate in discussions and add value by answering questions. You can also start conversations and ask questions which raises your profile within the group.

One of the great advantages of being in a group is that you can connect with people in that group directly. When you ask someone to connect on LinkedIn they make sure you know him by asking if you have done business together or if you are friends, and if you have not or are not, then you need to know his email address. People also allow you to connect if you are common members of the same group and that way you don't have to know their email addresses to connect.

Because of this, if you want to connect with someone directly but you don't know her yet you can join one of the groups she is in (look at her profile page to see which ones) and then use that to reach out and link with her. Once linked, you can then direct message her to start a conversation.

The other way to use groups effectively is to start your own. When I had the social media business I started a group for professionals who wanted to learn more about social media for business, i.e., my prospective audience. It started off slowly but pretty soon it reached over 100. Now the group has over 700 members, and I don't know what to do with it now, as it is not my business anymore but because I am a nice guy, I keep the group running as there are some great discussions on there.

Maybe you can start a group for your prospective and current clients. You can be blatant and just set up a user group for your services if that works for you or you can set one up for your subject area. Refer back to the education part of this book for ideas on how to best tackle the subject areas which will suit your audience the most.

You can have an open group which allows anyone to join or a closed group where you moderate the members. I suggest a closed group as you don't want recruiters and spammers in there messing up the experience.

General LinkedIn Do's and Don'ts:

On LinkedIn you can build a company page if it your responsibility to do so. You can add content to this page also and people can follow you as a company, so it is worth spending time on it. Make sure everyone in your organisation is connected to the page and make sure it looks professional and has the right logo, etc.

If you have Facebook and Twitter accounts for your business then you can link them together with LinkedIn and share comments and updates in much the same way. If you have a blog you can integrate your blog into your LinkedIn profile, which is useful for news updates.

Your updates are important and they must be:

- Relevant
- Interesting
- Informative
- Educational
- Often humorous
- Never too pushy—you can sell but in an informative way
- Be true to what you are like as a person, do not pretend to be someone you are not, people see through it very quickly
- Relevant to you and your audience, become known for what you know

You need to build your network on LinkedIn and it takes time. Make sure you connect with people who are relevant to you. You should take time to have a look around the site and see what is available, as it is constantly changing and developing.

Other Web Sales Tools

There are a huge array of tools available to sell your product directly online, but to sell yourself as a credible authority is your key to your personal sales success. LinkedIn is great, but there are other ways of getting your voice out there.

Some salespeople start a blog as themselves (have a look at mine http://www.21stcenturyselling.co.uk/) and they blog about their particular expertise. If you are in a large corporation check with your IT department first. A good friend of mine is in recruitment sales and he started a blog on how to find great talent and much to his surprise, it took off. He got a lot of business from it because it was interesting and it engaged his audience.

Twitter is also a good tool for you as a professional, as you can link it to LinkedIn and you can post up interesting things you find, as you are now continuously educating yourself. You can separate your business and professional profile effectively if you like, but common sense is needed to make sure it is appropriate.

If there are forums for your industry or your clients' industries, then spend time on these and add value as I mentioned earlier in the book. You can quickly set yourself up as an expert and refer to your postings and your blog for that matter in meetings if your prospects want to know more.

If you get a chance to write articles for online publications, then take them and shout about it. These are great for raising your credibility and you can get a lot of leverage out of this if you are clever about it. I have written several articles this year and they have been published online, in print and on blogs. I have shared them with clients and prospects and tweeted about them and shared the links on LinkedIn, it has brought us at least one large partner that I know about.

So in essence, do not ignore the web, use it to your advantage and make sure that you have a credible and sustainable online presence professionally. Use it to reach out and educate your audience and network. Be targeted and be niche, as niche on the web builds an audience.

This first section has concentrated on how to get in front of people. The next section now will concentrate on how to maximise your time in front of them when you meet.

Section 2

How to Set the Deal Up and Close It

Face to Face Pitch – Where Most Get it Completely Wrong

Strategic selling gets you in the room, and technique keeps you there.

So far I have covered how to get connected with people and what to say to them to get them to a place of trust so you can then take the sales process to the next stage. That is strategic. Mostly in professional selling the next stage is a face to face meeting. I appreciate that many of you will not do face to face meetings, but as you will see, most of the information I cover here is very applicable to all types of sales situations, so read on.

As I sit here I am struggling to remember the number of really good, competent sales meetings I have been in where I was the audience or an onlooker. It is so hard to find sales professionals who are outstanding at this, which is strange considering it is not that hard to do really well. Face to face sales has a lot to do with mind-set, which will be covered later in detail later, but for this part let us see what techniques you can implement to make your meetings achieve a much higher success rate.

Of all areas of sales, I enjoy this the most and so this is probably my strongest area. I love being with people, and I love getting them from a cold, distant place to engaged and excited about what we are discussing. Do you love it or is it all very difficult and daunting? If it is the latter, then have no fear. Just follow these simple rules and you can master it.

Prep, Prep, Prep

This is not always possible, especially if you sell through partners and it is their meeting you are attending, but if it is your meeting and you are in charge, then you have to do your homework before you set a single foot through the door.

The first thing to consider is that you are the one in charge of the meeting, you control the environment and you control the tempo, rhythm and outcome of the meeting. If you are meeting at your prospect's offices, then your goal must be at least to achieve parity in this. If you can, try to get the meeting in a neutral location, like a coffee shop or third party offices. Better still, do it at your offices and if you have a kit to demonstrate then this could be used as a good excuse to take the meeting to you.

When the meeting is at your office you can control all the elements; when the meeting is at their place of work they feel more comfortable and in charge. I appreciate that this may be obvious but it seems to be overlooked more often than not. These days, people are more favourable to having meetings (especially one to one) which are in any one of the millions of coffee shops in every town. I like these locations as they allow you to be in control. You can set the location, time and you can buy the drinks, pick the table and set the tone, none of which you can do at their place.

Once the location is set you must spend time, at least mentally, to completely understand what your goal is. It is astonishing to me how many people I see who do not have a very clear objective for the meeting. If I ask them, all I get as a reply is, "to take it to the next part of the sales process," or "let's see how it goes," or worse still, "to see if they are interested."

If the objective of the meeting is to see if they are interested or not, then a face to face meeting is not the place to do it. From my calculations, if I go to a meeting it costs my company about $500. The cost is based on total expenditure: my salary, other work lost and so forth. So if it costs that much I had better be going to a meeting which is unbelievably well qualified. I would far rather not go to an unqualified meeting than waste $500 and my time. How often to do you go to unqualified meetings or wasted meetings where you were surplus to requirements or the other person in the room was not the right person, or the conversation was not what they or you expected?

Too many people are scared to properly qualify meetings and ask the right questions in the first place. They believe that they may "blow out" the prospect if they push too hard on the difficult questions prior to a face to face meeting. We all know that this is not true, that real prospects do not blow out easily and that they would respect you more if you treated them with the respect they deserve and you command by being honourable with your and their time. Do not be afraid to qualify people out of your sales process; this will save you a lot of time and wasted energy. Spend time with the people who want you to be there and not with the people who agreed to see you because you and they "think" you may have something of value to them.

I always confirm the meeting before I set off, normally a day or two before. Yes, this allows the other person to reschedule or blow you out and, as said above, this is a good thing and it saves your time. If they do this you can at least try and qualify it back in.

If another organisation gets the appointments for you then definitely confirm the appointment, as many times these are not set correctly. This also allows you to reconfirm the expectations of the meeting, location, time and list attendees, reconfirming that the meeting and its details sets the expectation in the mind of the prospect that you are professional, thorough and that you value your time.

Alongside making sure you are ultra-clear on your objectives for the meeting, also make sure that you have done your homework. Here are some ideas to assist:

- Check out the profile of the attendees on LinkedIn (they will also see, if they are looking, that you have viewed their profile).
- Check out their website, especially their client testimonials, and all the more obvious details such as employees, management team, locations and so forth.
- Any related news articles to their company, you can comment on these in the meeting.
- Who their biggest competitors are and what they are doing in your space.

Sure, you may know these things to do, but do you do them every time and have you been caught short in a meeting because you did not prep properly in the past? I know I have! Get used to being incredibly detailed about this, as it will win you credibility, rapport and deals.

The Top Five Things to Do in Face to Face Meetings

Now we get to the crux of it. This is where the rubber meets the road. As there is so much to potentially cover, I thought I would make it easy for you and just do the top five areas to excel in so you can soak it in and get it right whilst keeping it simple.

1. Set Yourself Up for Success From the Start

First things first: dress for success! I have a rule that is I will always dress one level up from my audience as it makes me look more professional. So for example if it is a first meeting I will always wear a tie even if I know that the culture in their business is that they don't. I often wear three-piece suits and pocket handkerchiefs, as my view is you cannot look too professional or well dressed. However, you also want to be relatable, so the one level up rule applies. If I am going to a media company for example and I know they wear jeans I won't wear a tie but I will wear a suit. For my second meeting and beyond then I will dress more like them so we can relate, but first impressions matter (and you don't get a second chance).

The next area that is very often overlooked is the "who sits where" at the table. These are the essential principles to follow:

Make sure you do not create a "them and us" scenario with three of them are on one side of the table and three of you on the other, for example, mix it up instead. Control the room, as best you can, by choosing which seat you want to be in. If you can sit at the head of the table, more the better. If you are going with a partner or introducer and they have settled onto one side of the table then sit on the same side as the prospect as it makes you look like you are on their side.

Sit adjacent to the main person in the room if you can, as it makes you look like peers and if that is not possible, sit in the middle of the other side opposite them. You want to be able to relate to them directly as the meeting progresses with specific interaction between the two of you, so you will need to be up close and personal. Basically don't be at the opposite end to the decision maker; get close.

If they offer you a drink, take it as people like to be hospitable and if you can go with them to make it then do so, as it has been a great opportunity for me many times to say "I'll come with you and give you a hand," on the journey to start to create rapport.

As I said earlier, if you can get a neutral location or have the meeting at your offices then even better as it allows you to control the whole environment from temperature to seating positions. Remember, you are in charge here and you are the one directing the proceedings.

Also as you sit, notice who is where, make sure you look in detail at their business cards (especially if they are Japanese!) when you get them and make a note of everyone's name. If there are a lot of people in the room I draw a map and put people's names on it so if I need to reference them by name, I can.

2. Get Rapport Quickly (People Do Business With People They Like and Trust)

Rapport is the single most important thing in successful sales. Not only in getting the sale but in keeping the customer long term. Without it, you will get, more than likely, nowhere. I have seen it so many times where the sale was made because the prospect just liked the person. Yes better looking people have a higher success rate of closing deals (especially, I am afraid to say, in this sexist world, women) but over the long term rapport is what makes the difference between winning and losing— fact!

So how do you create it in a face to face meeting? Well first, be likeable. People like people who are like themselves, so speak like they do and at the pace they do and the pitch they do. Sit like they do and try to move at the pace they do. If you run it at 100 miles an hour speaking at 300 words a minute and the prospect is a country reared, slower talking, considered individual, then they simply won't relate to you and probably won't like you either.

Take some time to see what they are like and ask the usual open-ended questions first. Also, try not to jump straight in to the sale; talk about them and see what interests them first if you can. If they jump straight in then you know what they are like and you can be like them and get on with it.

Also try and compliment something, anything—be it the room, office, pictures, their suit, I don't mind, just make them feel good and make them feel good quickly. Chances are that they are in a rush, hassled and thinking about other things, so get their attention and be nice.

Also if you can pull it off, be funny. Humour works amazingly well. Do not be a joker, but if you can be humorous and witty quickly, people will like you more. If you are not naturally funny, then please don't try it, it will backfire.

One last but very important thing on rapport, please stop saying "thank you for your time." You may think this is rude and that you are not like that but if you say that or "thank you for coming," then it puts you below your prospect and psychologically they start to believe that their time is more precious than yours and that they are above you. They are not, and you are equals.

It grates me a lot to hear sales professionals almost begging as they thank people and it looks and sounds weak and desperate. Please don't do it. Say things like "pleasure to meet you" or "good to see you and I enjoyed our conversation" or "I hope you found our meeting as productive as I did."

I talk a lot more about attitude later, but your attitude needs to be that you have a lot to offer (this bit does not read well) and you can really do them a favour.

3. Feeling the Room and Sensory Acuity

As the meeting progresses you have to rise above it sometimes and see what is really going on, see and sense what is happening. Too often we get stuck in a track and patter along and we don't look up. Full flow is good, but only if the room is coming with you. Check in with yourself every now and again to see how it is going. Are you still on track? Are your goals being met? Most important, is everyone engaged with what is happening?

I was in a sales pitch recently where there were two of us pitching, myself and a technical person who claims to be a good salesperson. About 30 minutes into the meeting as the other person was drawing everything on a whiteboard and racing off down the full blown pitch, I noticed that the main decision maker looked uncomfortable and disengaged, so I had to stop my colleague full flow and ask what was wrong. Sure enough, it turned out that what he thought was happening was a show stopper which we never could have recovered from if we have not addressed it right then and there. I stopped the pitch and we clarified the issue and then changed the pitch to accommodate his concerns.

It is so easy to get into a flow, especially if your pitch is a well-rehearsed presentation which you have done a thousand times; it can take you into automatic pilot which is dangerous. Make sure you keep on the ball and engage with everyone in the room at all times and make sure that they are still with you. Look at their body language and facial expressions—are they taking notes or doodling? I kid you not, once I fell asleep in a one to one meeting where someone was pitching me and I don't think he even noticed!

Do not be afraid to stop and ask what is wrong and pull people up on their behaviour. Change the room temperature or do something different if you are losing the room. Make sure that you have enough sensory acuity (the ability to make sensory discriminations to identify distinctions between different states or events) to see when things need to be changed or challenged. Often I stand up and draw things on whiteboards or flipcharts just to change the energy and flow of the meeting.

Part of this is also about not wasting your time, and a few times in meetings I have had to requalify the interest as basically nobody looked interested. We have either then drawn the meeting to a close or answered questions which were lingering. There is no point in sitting there a moment longer if what you have is not what they want; get out and move on if you need to.

Most important, please listen to the question if they ask one. NOT the question you wish it was or thought they were going to ask but the actual question they asked. This may sound incredibly sales 101, but so many times I have had to either ask "do you mean this or that" to the questioner to clarify what I was being asked. Or what I find really annoying, stopping a colleague mid-sentence because they have clearly misunderstood the meaning of the question. At best, this annoys the questioner and at worst they will think you don't understand and you don't care, and because you don't care, you will have lost the most important thing, rapport.

Spend time practicing rising above the meeting and reviewing what is happening. Read books on body language and building rapport. Be humble and understand that everyone needs to be better at this, that you don't know everything and that you are not perfect. If you find yourself saying "I don't do that" then you are really in trouble! Please pay attention to what is really going on and not what you think is going on.

4. Be in Charge and Be the Expert

It is all too easy to let a face to face meeting get away from you. If your prospect is a strong personality and an alpha male then you may need to box clever to show yourself as an equal. The key here is showing yourself as an equal, not making the other person look bad by you beating them to death with your knowledge.

As quickly as I can, in a relaxed way, I try to establish myself as the authority on what I am talking about. I use the "did you know" information we discussed earlier and I use examples and certain really detailed technical sentences to prove my mettle. This should be done in an educational way and with an attitude of "I am here to help you, which will really make a big difference to your life and to what you do." I definitely suggest you take time to educate them as your primary focus, as this establishes you as the expert and allows you to gain parity.

Initially is not the time to talk about prices, benefits or features. First make sure they understand what is going on in the field you are there to discuss. Help them understand what organisations are doing in their sector to get ahead and give real examples of things you will do to make that happen if you can. Teach them about what is going on, trends and market changes, not buttons and switches.

Once you have established your credibility and your understanding of the market, then you can move on to what everyone else starts with, but with the distinct advantage that you are now the one seen as the credible supplier.

This, however, is worthless unless you have rapport. Let me explain with an example:

About a year ago I made a mistake in a face to face meeting which you should never do. In the meeting was the IT manager of a large legal firm and the introducer of my firm, which was managing their office move. In all there were 5 people in the room at the start, four of us and the IT manager. During the meeting it became clear that the IT manager was only really interested in empire building and protecting his job, and as I progressed with what I was trying to tell him, it was evident that he was not interested in change even though what I was discussing would have really helped him and his team. I got more and more annoyed with him and it showed. Because I was annoyed, I tried to give more and more detail about what I knew and how it could help him.

In an effort to assert my authority and establish myself as an expert so he would at least see me as an equal (absolutely critical when dealing with technical people), I pushed far too hard on the point I was trying to make and he closed up even more. Later in the meeting his boss came in so I tried to make the same points to him but he was not technical and looked to the IT manager for the nod and it never came!

I did not take enough time to understand his world first and establish rapport so even though it was clear that I knew my subject, he did not care as he did not see me as an equal who was interested in his objective, which was as little change as possible.

The process should be in this order:

1. Rapport
2. Educate
3. Technical detail

Not the other way around. Needless to say, we did not get the deal and I learned a valuable lesson. If you find yourself in the same situation in a meeting where the main technical purchaser is losing interest, you can do several things:

- You can close the meeting out and go above his or her head (this is your worst option as they will only scupper you later).
- Walk away and look for opportunities where you can make a mark.
- Spend all your time building rapport and agreeing with them which makes them feel important. This will take time and maybe a few meetings but it is your best route. In my experience, technical people often just want to be seen as right and knowledgeable, so if they get that validation they may come around to your way of thinking.
- Manufacture the situation to make them think that the idea was their idea. Often when they feel threatened, actually helping them come to the same conclusion as you but from their angle

works. This takes quite a bit of skill and experience but this is probably your best chance of success. You have to know their real goals and drivers to achieve this.

Of course there are many ways to skin this cat but these are your main ones. Appearing as the expert to the final decision makers is always your best option as they can use you to validate their decisions which you told them about in the first place.

So take control of the meeting, make your mark and make sure that it continually goes in the direction you want. I appreciate that sometimes it is not your meeting, but at least for your section of it, be the boss and stamp your authority on it.

4. Bring a Pen and After

Of all the ways to improve your sales in this area, this is the most critical.

How you close out a meeting is vital to your success. Often the end is left as a weak, limp noncommittal event. Every scenario is different and your outcomes from a meeting will always differ depending on your industry, audience, product sales cycle and so forth. However, here are some critical points which are universal.

Know your objective up front – what do you want out of the meeting? What is the next step in your sales process? Do you know your sales process in order to be able to define what your next step is? Can you take your potential clients on a journey which you design, which gives them what they want and which also give you what you want? If you are looking for a signature, bring a PEN and a contract!

I heard of a meeting the other day from a colleague where at the beginning of the meeting the lady in reception said, "You have come on a good day, he is in a signing mood!" and sure enough at the end of the meeting he asked for the contract to sign. Did the salesperson have it on it him? Sadly, no!

For crying out loud, if your goal is to get a yes, make sure you can at least get a commitment from them if they say yes, and be prepared to move it on to the next stage quickly.

This is not a chapter about closing, and actually I am not going to do one (maybe in my next book). However, it never hurts to be reminded of the basics.

Make sure you get specific actions from them (and your side too) for the next stage and agree on timescales before you close out the meeting. Too often I have seen—and been guilty of myself— leaving a meeting with, "I will be in touch," or "Let's catch up soon." This is nowhere near good enough. Get dates, times, commitments and an agreement to move forward.

It is always best for you to have actions from a meeting so you can then have a reason to be in touch. If the buyers are the ones with all the actions, you will be waiting for them, and they are now in control, which is not good.

If they are not committing to anything at least get them to commit to a follow up call with a time and date. Next week sometime is not good enough. It is always a good sign to see people with their diaries out at the end of a meeting; it shows progress.

Do not let a meeting drag on too long. Keep it lively and fast paced. If the audience is a laid back, slow talking type then of course mimic them, but still you can keep the pace and the flow of the meeting on track. Don't get bogged down in details which are of no consequence to your outcome. Remember, you are in charge.

Please also do not oversell. If you have a yes, then seal the deal and stop talking.

So know your purpose for the meeting, get actions from both sides, know your next steps and communicate them. Keep the sales flow going and make sure you retain control of the process.

What Should You Accept as Rude?

There still seems to be, generally speaking, a dim view of salespeople—a view that we are there to sell something people don't need at a price they don't want to pay for it. Because of this, many sales professionals still have the attitude of subservience and a demeanour that they need to beg for business and go with cap in hand to get it! Obviously if you believe in what you do, then there is no need for this, but still at some level society still treats us like second class citizens who are lazy and greedy. To me, this is not acceptable and it should not be to you either.

There are certain things I do not like or accept in meetings, or when meeting someone or a group of people. I am sure there are many things you struggle with, too. Some are listed below with suggestions showing you how I deal with them. You may agree or disagree with the actions I take and you can do the same; however, if you don't it is the mental attitude which is key.

My attitude is that my time is at least as valuable as my prospect's time and actually in fact to me, it's more valuable. I don't like being messed around with, and my experience is that if someone messes you around once then that is their pattern and they will do it again.

As I said earlier, I do not believe in the adage that you should not call to confirm a meeting before the meeting as it gives the person the chance to blow you out. So what if they do? There is only a small chance that if you call up they will do this as long as the meeting was set up correctly in the first place.

I have found that if they do blow you out, actually you can agree to move the date to a more suitable time. Then they owe you one and they are already more grateful to you for helping them out. Also you don't want to have them blowing you out on the day of the meeting which really messes you around. Be strong when confirming. Not having time is not a great excuse but rescheduling is better than a pressed-for-time meeting where all they want to do is get out of the room quickly.

If they do blow you out and they don't want to reschedule, then either you were wasting your time anyway or you should find out why and press forward for a meeting regardless.

Your time is precious and you don't want to waste it with inappropriate, unqualified meetings where the audience does not want to be there. The number of times where you can turn that around is so few that in the general scheme of things it is better to work with the prospects who want to be worked with and not cajoled.

When you turn up for a meeting, how long do you give the prospect before you walk out if he is late? Do you even have a rule for that? Mine is 30 minutes, and so far nobody has breached it. I may bring it down to 20 soon as I believe that more than 15 minutes late is rude without a valid reason.

An old boss of mine had a meeting with a huge prospect, and after 20 minutes the people did not appear so he walked out! I cannot remember how it ended but it did not matter to me; the lesson is the same, value your time.

I remember many years ago waiting for a large prospect with a business partner and they forgot we were coming so we waited for ages. The person I was with made me wait for what in the end was a rushed meeting born out of guilt by the prospect, and of course we never won the business and we were never going to. If the meeting was not set up right then we would never have made a sale but actually if the person is just plain rude, then I don't want to deal with her and neither should you. If you feel strongly when you are messed around with also, you may want to make a complaint about them so that in the future they treat the next sales professional with more courtesy and dignity.

How do you handle interruptions and mobile calls? I was in a sales meeting about a year ago when the person I was in the meeting with (there were three of us) answered his phone and said, "No, it's OK, I can talk." Now as I am a decent person, I did not say anything but on reflection, I should have said nothing, packed my bag up and left. Next time I will! Needless to say we did not do any business.

What are your tolerances for these situations? It does matter, as how you handle these issues sets you up for success or failure, and is a reflection on who you think you are professionally. Do you see yourself as a sales professional who adds value or a salesperson who nobody wants to see?

You must be polite but firm, do not let people get away with it. If people do not value your time, move on.

Presentations – the Art of Boredom

I was on a train recently when a teenager reminded his friend that, "Back in the day you couldn't get pictures on Snapchat." That is not back in the day—that was last year! Back in the day for me is about 1995!

Anyway back in the day (about 1995) was when I saw my first presentation using PowerPoint. For the last twenty years or so, things have not really changed that much. Sales professionals still use PowerPoint to affect great boredom and seem to be generally sticking to the same old methods I saw back in the day.

Steve Jobs was the master of presentations and I would highly recommend the book, "The Presentation Secrets of Steve Jobs" by

Carmine Galio. Pick up a copy. However, assuming you do not have the budget or presentations skills of Jobs, then read on.

If you feel that you have to use a PowerPoint or equivalent, then these pointers will help you.

First, include a picture on every slide. Many people think in pictures, not words, so a good chunk of your audience will be lost if you only use words. Make the pictures interesting and relevant. I use Google Images and www.istockphoto.com to get mine and all I would say on that is make sure you don't infringe any copyright laws when obtaining yours.

A more favourable form of presentation for me is the Ashton Kutcher method of presenting which is more fun and inventive. The rule is seven slides in seven minutes, and pictures only. This means that you have only one minute per slide and one picture to describe what you are explaining. This is a great idea if you are getting salespeople to interview for you, by the way. Get them to present in this style for you as their pitch of themselves. If salespeople can't present, they can't sell in the real world.

Use as few words on every slide as you can get away with. Still make your point but do not over crowed the slide so people cannot read it and as I have seen many times, they spend more time trying to read the presentation than listening to the presenter—not good. Also make sure it can be read easily from the back of the room.

Make the presentation snappy, energetic and as brief as you can. Make sure you cover everything you really need to but keep the energy high and the length down. You do not want them falling asleep and snoring through your pitch; personally I would take this as a "no" if they do!

As I stated earlier in the book, opening with the history of your company and who you are is not a good start. You need to blow their socks off. Use your "did you knows" from earlier, use graphs to illustrate your points on what trends are happening which affect them. They don't generally care who you are, they just want to know that you know what you are doing and you know what you are talking about. If they want to ask you about your company later, they will.

Grab yourself a clicker which interacts with your presentation to move the slides forward and backward. It is frustrating to see presenters having to run across the room and press a button on their laptop to move the presentation on. A clicker like this one,

Is available on the web for a small amount and will help you look more professional and slick. Also make sure that it has a make the screen blank button as you will need this. I use the make the screen blank when I have an important point to make. I don't want the audience staring at the screen when they should be looking at me. You can also flip back quickly to earlier slides if you need to, which is very handy. Also it avoids the embarrassing-slide-appearing-on-your-face-moment when you are standing in front of the projector.

I do not see this that often, but if you do this then please stop. Please do not read from a card or read your presentation from a sheet word for word, it's terrible. Make sure you know the slides really well, especially the one coming next. It should not be a shock to you when the next one pops up. Use some guidance notes if you have to but only as guidance, practice until you know it like the back of your hand, no exceptions. If you know your subject very well and you are confident at speaking then this will not be an issue for you.

Use consistent slide design. It is well worth having a designer work on your company template, which you can use forever. If you are a small company then you can do this very inexpensively and if you are part of a larger corporate then you should already have one from your marketing department, so please use it. Seeing the standard stock designs from Microsoft on your presentation is not cool.

If you do not feel that you are as polished as you should be with presenting, then I suggest you take at least one course, and if you can, join the speaker's guild or a speaking group so you can practice at becoming outstanding at it. This skill is absolutely critical for sales regardless of who you are and how you sell.

Hopefully these pointers will help you brush up on your skills and give you some easy things to remember during your next pitch.

If I am forced to present like this then fine, I will use this template to make it work; however, this is absolutely not my preferred method.

Depending on the size of the audience, and remembering that in a pitch there probably won't be more than 10 people, I like to draw things out and explain what we can do. What I sell on a day to day basis is reasonably technical so I can do this using pictures and drawings with small lists of words.

If I can, I ask for a flip chart or whiteboard to be in the room and at least 4 coloured pens (or I bring my own). During the presentation I then demonstrate what we do by drawing up a scenario on the board which is different every time, as it depends on the audience, but it does follow the same structure. I write lists of things to remember and critical points summed up in a few words which help the audience to focus on what is important.

This allows for many things. It allows me to tell a story and bring the prospect from where they are now to where I want them to be. It allows me to make certain key points with colour and I use the pens to point at the most important words or part of the drawing.

Most important, presenting this way also engages the audience. What I have found over the last few years of doing this is that when prospects sit through presentations, there seems to be an unwritten rule about not asking questions until the end. When I draw on a whiteboard or flipchart they get more involved and a discussion rather than a sermon takes place and ideas flow. It seems more real to them and they can get involved. This leads to more engagement and a spirit of collaboration rather than a pitch.

It also allows me to show the audience that I know my craft, industry and product and I can adapt the presentation to suit my audience on the fly which is almost impossible when using slides.

If the audience is large then this may not be the most suitable form of presenting for you, but I have used it for up to 20 in the room.

My main point here is that it is often better to be different than better and if you follow the way of the crowd and your competitors, then you will look like all the rest. Try and think how you can weave your pitch into a drawing presentation rather than a static slide-driven one, and practice it to see how you get on.

If no whiteboard or flipchart are available, then you may have to keep the slides in your back pocket as a backup. You can also try a hybrid and use both if that works for you.

Many times these days, however, I find that sales pitches do not need a full blown presentation, as they are discussions around the table. You do not need to be good at drawing or writing at all, in fact many times mine is a mess by the time I have finished. So play with it and see how you get on. Just please do not be dull.

Follow Up and Nail It

If you have a great pitch and you believe you have nailed it, how are you on following it up effectively to make sure that momentum is carried forward? I have been very guilty in the past of letting this go, moving on to the next prospect and sometimes forgetting to keep active track of the recent ones, which is not acceptable.

It costs a lot of money to do a pitch. First there is the time to set it up and do it, not to mention the marketing and pre-sales which got you in the room in the first place. It is all a massive waste unless you follow up correctly.

Do you have a written strategy for following up on prospects? Do you use a CRM tool like Microsoft Dynamics or Sales Force to track for you? Even if you are a one man army, I suggest that you use a CRM package to keep track of your prospects.

The first rule of following up is to do something quickly. If you have an action from the meeting which can be completed that day or the day after, then do it. You need to show that you are efficient and you do what you say you are going to do.

If you do not have an action which can be completed quickly, then at the very least send a follow-up email or better still, a letter, stating the agreed upon actions, next steps and maybe some observations from the meeting. It is not a chance to beg for the business or put pressure on the sale, it is a chance to continue the timely, prompt and efficient sales process. Show off how attentive you are and that you understand their needs and that you are doing something about it.

It is always a good idea to book a second meeting while you are still in the room, if you need a second meeting. I appreciate that this is not always possible, so maybe you can get two or three dates off them which suit, so you can firm one up later.

There should ALWAYS be a next action. Unless they sign there and then (in which case you have to deliver anyway!) you should always have something to do to move it forward. Never accept that all you are going to do is leave it hanging. If a follow-up call is required, much like the next meeting, get a time and date in the diary so you and they can commit to making it happen.

Make sure the interest remains high by providing useful information in the days and weeks afterwards. If you can, one of the best examples of this is sending over either some useful information on their industry which is not relevant to your pitch. Send it saying, "Hi, I found this article/ post/ site and thought you would find it useful." Do not talk about your dealings with them; just genuinely offer it as a piece of standalone useful information.

Better still, if they have divulged some piece of personal information during your dealings, you can use that to continue the rapport. For example maybe their daughter plays hockey for the local team, have a look around for something they would like to know or see and send that. Show that you care about them and that you are keen on building a relationship. Do not be fake or underhanded, this is not a tactic to manipulate, it should be a genuine act of kindness and assistance.

Above all, make sure you follow up until you get your next milestone on your process, then follow up after that until the next, and so on. Do not let things slip or they will think that you have stopped caring about them and their needs. Keep going until you get what you want.

Define your sales process and follow up strategies. Understand how long your sales lead time is and measure it. You cannot measure your pipeline unless you know how long it takes to convert a lead into a sale. Use real data, not anecdotal gut feel information, which will be wrong.

So to wrap up the message is to keep the conversation going, don't be too pushy but stay in their psyche and keep yourself as the credible educator in their mind. You should be the one they call when they have a general question about what your industry does, and nobody else. Become their trusted advisor during the whole process and you will win the business.

So far we have discussed how to get you in the door and what to do when you get there. Now I am going to cover the most important part in making you more successful than you can imagine.

Section 3

How to Set Yourself Up for Success

The Keys to Selling More and Becoming the Best

Selling on Price (Strategic v Tactical)

I hear so many times from sales professionals who believe that they need to be selling on price. They become fixated with it and it rules their sales lives. One thing is for sure, if you sell on price then you are on a path to ruin. At some point there will always be someone cheaper than you and in technology, for example, many companies sell at below cost in order to achieve targets or to sell their base, so you cannot compete with that. So don't.

Selling on price even, if you believe you are in a commodity industry, is not the way forward. Let me give you an example:

Many years ago I looked after the telecoms for a large paper manufacturer. I saved them a lot of money and brought a great deal of value. They trusted me to educate them and help them. Every year, though, they would still look at the market to benchmark prices and offerings. One particular year a large competitor offered them crazy rates, way below market averages. They would have been remiss to ignore it, so they asked for my opinion. They had already made the decision to move and I was about to lose the account.

After a long discussion where I was getting nowhere, I asked them one simple question, "If you could not receive or make any calls in your business, how long do you think you would last?" Remember that they made paper, they were not a call centre or a bank. The answer that came back still amazes me. The answer was 48 hours! They fully believed that they would have to shut down a 150-year-old company if they could not make or receive calls for 48 hours. They thought they were buying a commodity when in fact they were purchasing a critical element of their business.

Needless to say I retained the account because they wanted to keep their business with a trusted partner who looked after them. Sure, I did a rate reduction to assist. We worked together for several years after this event.

So even if you think that you are in a highly competitive price driven market, you need to differentiate yourself. If you do that then you will win more business.

Adding value is the best way to get away from the price discussion. If you add enough value you will be surprised as to people's loyalty. I have discussed at length in this book about adding value and education and if you implement all I have gone through, then you will find that you are fighting fewer price battles.

Sure, you need to be competitive and you cannot rip people off, but as long as you are within the normal realms of what people expect to pay based on the market, then adding value will be enough to win. There are prospects who are completely fixated on costs and I get that some will not be swayed. If you run into these people and you cannot win on price, then move on!

Recently at a sales training course I was presenting, one of the delegates would not move from price as his question. He could not see how adding value was the key. I politely answered his several questions relating to this discussion and eventually he got so fixated that it was interrupting the flow of the training, so it had to be put to bed.

His belief was that "his" clients only cared about price and that the area of the market he sold into was only interested in price. So we went through how he could change that perception. By the end I do believe he got it and interestingly a very important point came out of the discussion, so we all learned.

The point was that if he helped companies improve anything else in their business, productivity, customer complaints, communication, reducing staff, improvements in efficiency etc., then the total value of that was what needed to be measured, and not the cost of what they were buying. It seems obvious but most in the room agreed that they do not use this point to make sales.

When you next sit in front of a prospect or you are writing a proposal based on your offering, look at the whole picture from a cost point of view. Try to add up the actual tangible monetary value of the overall value you will provide and weigh that up against the cost of what you provide. Often companies argue over such small amounts that they fail to see the bigger picture. It is your job to get them back on track and see the whole rather than the isolation of their spend with you.

Let me give you a real and recent example of where adding value destroys the cost element.

One of our clients is a pharmaceutical company. It provides clinical trials for its drugs and needs to be in regular contact with its human guinea pigs. The problem was that when it called from overseas, the recipients of the call would not answer because they thought they would be charged to take the call. This resulted in the company having to send someone out to physically check the person to make sure he or she was alright.

We had a call with them and told them of the value we could add and the how we could solve this particular issue. I remember this very clearly—right at the end of the call the prospect said, "Oh, and how much does this cost?" He had made the decision and as long as we were not going to rip him off we had a sale. We solved his pain and added value and saved the business a lot of money. He didn't really care how much it cost and obviously we won the business. If we had gone in on price and not adding value, that conversation would never have happened as they already had a supplier they were happy with.

So add value; look for ways you can improve your client's business and educate them on how you can work together to achieve this. Fight on price and someday you will be out of the game. The choice is yours.

We were in Vietnam a few years ago and we were really enjoying the bartering and negotiation culture. We paid less for everything than the first price quoted, apart from one shop. It was a jewellery store and my lady really fancied a ring and necklace. So I went over to haggle as usual and the attendant pointed to a sign which read, "The price is the price is the price!" I will never forget it; we laughed and paid the full price. Do not be afraid to stick to your guns—if people want it, they will pay.

Be the Last One Standing

Professional business to business sales is not a sprint. Too often sales professionals are impatient and lack the fortitude to be in it for the long haul. Of course, too many give up at the first or second no; however, this is not about that—it is about having the consistency of will to see things through. Giving up because it is too hard is giving up when you are tested the most. The best accounts to win are the ones who test you to be a better you.

I discussed earlier the need for understanding who else is selling to your prospect. This is crucial to understanding the field of play. As you progress, your goal is to be the last one standing. They should be left with no choice but to choose you. Too often we settle for being one of three or two or ten. Your goal is not to be one of a few choices but to be the only choice.

How do you achieve that?

Of course your education, confirmation of value and proof of delivery all play critical roles, but assuming you have done a good enough job of that, often the rest is up to your attitude.

How good are you at being responsive, available and proactive? You need to be outstanding at all three. Who cares if a prospect emails you at 10:00 p.m.? If you can reply, do so and be quick about it. You need to prove that you really want this and that it means a lot to you. Hunger is what separates sales professionals at this level. The one who wants it most, gets it.

A continual attitude of "I am the best here," "I will win this business and I am the only choice," should be your mantras. I will discuss mental attitude in more detail later. However, with regard to being the last one standing you must be in it for the long haul.

Part of this is getting back to people when you say you will get back to them. Be persistent but not pushy, be there for them. If you put their needs before your own, then that will shine through and you will be the last one standing.

Please do not let the appearance of your competition knock you off your game. You need to know why you are better and demonstrate that. Think differently and if they are bigger than you, then you need to be strategic and not tactical. There is no point lining up against a heavyweight and going toe to toe; box clever and be ruthless.

Too many times I have lost business because I have been too distracted with other opportunities to give my complete attention. Spreading yourself too thin will definitely not help you in being the last one standing, as you will not be able to give the prospect the attention he deserves and expects. So chose your battles wisely and stick with it through thick and thin. Do not give up until you are absolutely certain that there is no way you can be his supplier of choice.

Don't Be Afraid of No

Part of being the last one standing is getting past a no or a series of no's.

Nobody likes to hear no. Often we take it personally and our fear of rejection is realised. There are many books written on how to get past no; some are too aggressive in my mind but well worth a read.

Not being afraid of a no comes from belief in what you do and how you do it. Sometimes no does mean no, but often it comes from a lack of understanding on the prospect's part, which is your fault.

If you are not the right fit and you have done your complete utmost to educate and add value and you can look in the mirror and say, "That was my best shot," and you still get a no, then move on. If none of that is correct, then you owe it to your prospect to apologise for your behaviour and set them straight.

Keep going until a no is a no. Your prospect may be scared or misinformed, or misunderstood something. There can be a million reasons for the no. You must understand what the no really means before you walk away. By this I mean the reason she has is usually not the first reason she'll give; keep digging and you will be surprised as to why she said no. Often it is not too late and if you truly understand what happened, you can at least make your decision on what to do.

Don't waste your time chasing lost deals. There are so many prospects and opportunities out there. Your time should be spent working with the people who want to work with you. "Next" is a very empowering word, and you should use it often.

If you sell a service or product which has a repeat or contract term then remember your "no's" and make sure you keep in touch with your client. The amount of clients I have regained years after they first rejected what I was offering is significant. In a previous life I won the business of a Formula One team and kept that business for years. However it took me over two years to win the business in the first place. They went to a competitor initially and I waited until the contract was up and then converted them.

During the time I did not have the business I kept in touch from time to time and I kept educating them about the market, so that when it became time to review, guess who was first on their list?

Building a database of your "no's" is a very important tool to building a pipeline for the future. Put them on your email marketing list. Keep in touch every so often and continue to inform and educate. Your job as educator is to educate every possible prospect. If you have approached the sale in a correct and diligent manner, then you have already done most of the hard work, so don't let that go to waste.

Saying that, do not be annoying or a pest. Short term aggressive sales is just that—short term. The shorter the sales cycle and the less repeatable the product or service, the more aggressive the approach. If you are in long term business to business sales or repeatable business to consumer sales, keep your reputation intact. You will be surprised how quickly you get a poor reputation for overly aggressive sales.

One last thing on this subject. If things go quiet during the sales process, be careful not to take this as a lack of interest. So many times I have asked salespeople what was happening with a prospect and they would say something like, "I haven't heard from him in a while, so it's dead." No, it is not dead until you have completed your task and heard a real "no." Never assume it is dead, ever.

Different Types of Buyers

Since the dawn of time salespeople have known that they need to get in front of decision makers as that is where the real influence occurs. Time and time again we have been told to seek them out and make sure that their buy-in is guaranteed so the sale is assured. How many times have you done this, only to lose the sale anyway?

If you are in the business to business sales profession then you will have to deal with different types of decision makers, job types and skill sets. Even though your audience may be the purchasing department, they may bring in finance, IT or legal to assist in the purchasing process. The decision maker can be not one but many people. Even if the final decision rests with one person you can be assured that they will seek guidance from others first.

Earlier I covered knowing your audience and doing your research on what they want and need. Here you need to understand your audience from the participants' personal and job role needs. This is critical to know for business to business sales.

For example in our industry we used to pitch to finance directors and managing directors as the conversation was all about cost reduction. Now our industry has to sell to IT directors and operation directors. Many salespeople in our industry have not made the transition successfully. They still sell on cost and they do not understand that the chief influencers on purchasing decisions in technology have changed.

The higher the ticket value, or the deeper the value to the business you offer, the broader the range of types of influencers you will have to deal with and work with.

If you look around a typical board room table and the functions represented, see who you need to work with to get your offering approved. Who can sideswipe you with a shake of the head because you have not engaged with them? Often you see IT directors killing a deal because finance thinks it is a good idea but the technical influencer (the IT director) feels threatened or not engaged, and often ill-informed. This is your issue to deal with; do not let an important influencer go uneducated on what you are looking to get done.

A great example is the issue the current crop of salespeople selling cloud IT services are having. As described above, IT people feel threatened by the move to cloud IT services because they wrongly believe that their function will be removed. In reality this is not the case, but I have seen with my own eyes deals get crushed because the business relies on the IT manager for guidance and he says no.

People protect their own kingdoms all the time. They engage in empire building and they have their own agendas and needs. Your job is to satisfy all of these for all the influencers who need to approve what you do. Sure, you can go above people's heads and get a sale, but you will be resented and it will be harder for your company with that account long term. There is nothing like satisfying all the roles in a business at once. If you do that, then you are with that customer for life!

One of the most efficient ways to do this is to pitch to a board. Ask to be given a slot at the next management or board meeting to state your case. The next best thing is to be put on the agenda and prepare a brief for your sponsor in the business to take in. Make sure your pitch or brief satisfies all functions that you affect in the business.

Spread your word around. Ask for meetings with other key people who you would normally not pitch to. Endeavour to cast your net far and wide in the company. If you believe that you only have to deal with the boss, then you are most probably not seeing the whole picture.

Remember the decision maker(s) come in all shapes and sizes so keep asking quality questions about what parts of the business you will affect and who needs to be involved to ensure your success.

Train Your Clients to Be More, Do More and Have More.

Once you have finally won an account, your job is not over. Especially if you sell through partners or into large corporates. Too many salespeople walk away after a deal, hand it over to the implementation team and move on to the next prospect. If your sales process is set up this way, you may well want to review and change it, and here is why …

The best source of new leads is your customer base. Do you ask them enough to help you get into their largest suppliers or clients? Do you ask them for a written referral or case study to show off your successful relationship? If not, then you must.

Asking for testimonials and referrals and case studies has three effects.

1. They give you credibility when approaching others in their industry or line of work.

2. They feel more committed to you long term because they have written down why they use you and how much they love you. People do not like going back on their word. The more you get from them in testimonials, the more engrained they are into you as an individual.

3. If they don't want to give one, you can find out what is wrong and fix it. If they are not a raving fan, then your role is to make them such.

A key part to this also, is them becoming part of your sales force on a long term basis. Over the years I have received a lot of really profitable introductions through clients time and time again. I have even received referrals and introductions from clients to their competition, so you never know. Your sales pitch is so much easier if the weight of credibility of an introduction is behind you.

Training your existing clients is also about creating champions internally. Having strong allies in a business long term can secure your place as a preferred supplier for years. If you move on after the sale and leave it to others on a strategic level (I get that you need a team to implement) then you miss an opportunity to keep the account forever. You miss the opportunity to gain referrals and you miss the opportunity to cross sell other services on an ongoing basis.

OK, so there are hunters and gatherers and you are better at one than the other. However, if you are a hunter like me then you need to become a great gatherer (account manager) as well. It does not mean you have to be drinking coffee with them every day, you need to be smart and work with them effectively and efficiently.

The larger the sale and the more you make from continual profit with a client, the better the gatherer you need to become. Or at the very least, hire great account managers who can back you up.

One tip I use for existing clients is to send them information they will find interesting or useful. Keep them informed. If you continue to be the source of education for them they will stay with you. The education process is continual. Obviously email shots and social media play a part here, but personal emails or letters work so much better. Make them feel important continuously and make them feel valued as a client.

The Five Mental Strengths of the Best Sales People

There are so many books written about mind-set, focus, confidence and so on out there. Make sure you read as many as you can. I am going to cover the five things I believe to be the most important for you as a salesperson.

Unshakeable Belief

Sure you have to believe in your product, service, company and colleagues, but do you really believe in yourself? Do you believe you are the best? I believe I am the best salesperson I have ever known. Now that may sound arrogant (and it is) but why would I not believe that? I also believe that I can win any deal and beat any other salesperson who comes up against me. If I don't, then I will be intimidated and lose deals. I know I said it was arrogant, but actually I hold it as an inner core belief and it shows up in everything I do. I don't push my weight around and I am not saying you need to be a bully or brash. I am saying you need that inner confidence that you are the best, and there has been no other like you before.

The question is how do you get this belief? It is simple actually. Self-talk is one of the easiest ways. Write down a list of reasons why you are the best, what makes you the best and read it often. Drill it into your subconscious mind. Your subconscious does not know the difference between the truth and a lie, so you might as well tell it something which will be of benefit to you.

Read the book "What to Say When You Talk to Yourself" by Shad Helmsstetter. It's an excellent, detailed book on how to use self-talk effectively.

Having that belief really will affect everything you do in sales. A calm, inner confidence comes of it and you will start to be able to hold your own in any situation. Things will not fluster you and you will be able to engage with more people at a higher level.

Without this belief you will inevitably come up against someone who has it and my money would be on them!

Ruthless Pragmatism

If you have watched House of Cards, you will recognise this phrase. I love it as it describes perfectly the attitude about a dog-eat-dog world. In sales you feed yourself and your family by winning deals. You must win to succeed, and no amount of sugar coating it will change that fact.

Let women (if you are a man) go through the door first, but do not let your competitors do the same. Winning is about looking after the client's best interest first and making sure they are aligned with yours.

Having an attitude of ruthless pragmatism allows you to see things as they really are, not just as you think they are. It's about understanding that others have their own agendas and needs, and being able to use those to get what you want. This may sound cold but actually it is not. Your goal is to look after the people who mean something to you, your loved ones and yourself. Do not let your competitors or other people who do not have your best interests at heart get in your way.

For example if you are in a company that does not value your sales skills, maybe management always puts you down—they change the goal posts and screw you over on commission – leave and move on to work with people who let you be your best. You are in charge of your destiny and you control your environment. Be pragmatic and see things how they are. Have the belief in yourself to find the best company to work with or even start your own. The amount of opportunity for great salespeople is unbelievable; just ask around and you will see how much your skills are valued in the marketplace.

Ruthless pragmatism also relates to the ability to walk away from deals if they do not fit your criteria. Only this week I rejected two (on paper anyway) great prospects because I could see that their interests were not aligned with ours and the hassle that would come from working with them would be too much. Work with the people and clients you want to work with; life is too short not to.

Never-Ending Learning

Educating your audience is critical to sales, but educating yourself is even more important if you want to be as successful as you can be. Reading, attending seminars, listening to CDs, and all manner of self-development tools are at your disposal.

Working on your skills with people is core to who you are personally and professionally. If you have not read "How to Win Friends and Influence People," I would certainly suggest you do. Sales is a people business, period. Becoming an expert in human behaviour, body language and patterns on how people behave and why they do what they do will drastically change your results.

Learning how to improve yourself and your relationships is not a one off process; it is a continual, never-ending process. Reading is one of the best ways to learn, and audio books are very efficient as you travel about. Instead of listening to the radio, why not put in a CD and learn, develop and grow?

Obviously reading sales books like this is essential and I applaud you for doing so. Anything by Jim Rohn or Zig Ziglar or Tony Robbins will help you, and reading often is the key. A little every day if you can spare twenty minutes all adds up, and you will be surprised by the results and how quickly they come.

Educate yourself constantly.

Chameleon Behaviour

Your ability to adapt to any given situation is, of course, a great life skill. In sales it is especially important, because as you know, things change all the time! Adapting to changing markets, the wants and needs of customers, products, competitors' offerings, prices and so on is everything in keeping you ahead of the game.

Studying and listening will tell you what is changing and why. However, the skill you need is to be always open to change and having the strength and courage to adapt to it. The reason I wrote this book was because I have seen too many salespeople stay where they were, never willing to adapt to changing environments and skill requirements.

One of the most critical ways in which you need to adapt quickly is how you behave in front of different people. We discussed mirroring earlier and mimicking, both essential to adapting to your audience. When you need to be the life and soul of the party, be that; when you need to be calm and reflective and considered, be that. Learn how to be thousands of different personalities and you will do very well indeed. People will relate to you and you will see things others miss.

When a prospect throws you a curve ball, how do you react? Do you get angry, upset or hurt? Do you remain resolute, strong and adaptive? Look critically at yourself the next time it happens and be honest—what do you really do when things change? There is no room for salespeople who don't change, just watch the film Glengarry Glen Ross to see how that manifests itself in a sales team.

A truly adaptive and flexible salesperson will be at the top of his game for the long term; make sure you are that person.

Be Happy

Nobody likes anyone who is miserable! In sales, a smile goes a long way and as people like happy people, you need to be a happy person. If something is troubling you—your love life, children, work etc., do not let affect your attitude. Be happy anyway, and at the very least fake it at some level. If you fake being happy, soon your brain makes you actually become happy, so why not give it a whirl?

Over the years I have met so many unhappy salespeople. They come in with a cloud over them. Nobody wants to do business with someone like that. It spirals, and before they know it they are out of a job.

Enthusiasm is infectious, so spread it around like it saves people's lives! Enthusiasm for what you do and sell will pass on very quickly and your belief will soon transfer to your audience. If you do this, objections like price soon disappear and people want to be in your gang as it makes them feel good.

Be happy and enthusiastic about everything you do and watch your sales rocket.

Nature or Nurture

There is always the debate about whether salespeople are made or whether they are born. What do you think? I have always believed I could do sales, and the other day at lunch with some colleagues one of them said, "Ah yes, but you are a salesman, you can sell anything; I am not like that."

My belief is that salespeople can be made. They have to want to sell, but they can be trained to sell. Actually everyone sells all the time. We sell to our spouse when we are courting. We sell to our kids nearly every day. We sell to our bank, our friends and almost everyone we meet, constantly.

There is a genuine issue with society and how it sees salespeople. It believes that they are pushy, status-grabbing, self-important, arrogant and self-centred. As we have seen, great salespeople are the opposite. Because of this, so many great salespeople never come into our industry because they are scared they need to be like that, and they don't.

Some of the best salespeople I have met do not even realise they are in sales. Checkout ladies in the supermarket, friendly bank tellers, lawyers, doctors, teachers and many more have sold me very well over the years. But I bet if you asked them whether they were in sales, they would disagree.

If you are looking to get into sales, then my advice would be to use your natural ability to be enthusiastic, friendly and honest, and the rest will follow. Sure you will learn techniques along the way, but the core of what you need you already have; just believe that you can do it. Also, the best sales are done when you are not necessarily actively selling. Your honesty shows through and if you are helping someone rather than selling to him per se, then you will be more effective than the vast majority of salespeople out there.

OK, so I hear you cry, "What about closing the deal—surely that comes from being a natural sales- person?" Well, not really. Closing comes from belief and a genuine willingness to help people, which is a natural talent in all of us and practiced in our daily lives.

Be yourself and make sure you stick to who you are, and you will do very well indeed. Try to manipulate and use false techniques on people and they will see straight through you. Keep their interests first.

This is why I believe women make better salespeople than men. They are better at communicating. They don't let their ego get in the way. They sense when things are not quite right and they read people better than we do. Unfortunately, in a male dominated business world, the only reason men generally have more success than women at closing is that they are often selling to egotistical men, who want to be opened by a woman and closed by a man, which is very sad.

One last thing on being a better you. Dress like you are about to meet the most important person you have ever met in your life, every day. Pay attention to the details—nice watch, wallet and shoes. Dress one level above your audience as I said earlier. It says everything about you, and just because business has become more relaxed about dress code over the last few years does not mean you have to be lazy. It matters.

Running an Outstanding Sales Team

Being a great salesperson is one thing; being a great sales leader is quite another. If you run a sales team then here are some critical things you should know.

As a leader your first role is to put everyone else before you. If you have to prove yourself as the top salesperson all the time, that is poor sales leadership. It is not about you getting all the plaudits, it is about your team getting all the plaudits.

Someone once told me, and I agree, that the mark of a great sales director or manager is to help everyone else on the team achieve his target first. Passing leads, helping in sales, coaching and mentoring are all necessary in achieving this.

You need to have a team of superstars who make you look good, so that in turn you look like one, not the other way around. The amount of egotistical, self-important sales directors I have met over the years would make your head boil. Often they are bullies who only think about themselves and how well they look in front of the board. This is a very quick way to ruin.

Hiring Superstars

To have a team of superstars you first need to hire them. What is your current hiring strategy for salespeople? Do you simply call your recruitment company, ask for some CVs and pick out of that? Sure, that works sometimes, but you should also be looking out for salespeople all the time as you go about your busy day.

Have you ever run into a great salesperson in a shop or in a café? A waiter perhaps, or a bartender? What about them? If you can sell, you can sell, and if she is great with people she can sell! Try not to look from within your industry, as it is often better to start with a blank sheet of paper whom you can train and mould into the superstar she is destined to become.

However you find the raw talent, even if it is experienced, there are certain things to look out for.

Firstly make sure she can present. If someone cannot present she cannot be the best salesperson. Sure you can teach her how to present but if she lacks the basic belief that she can do it then do not waste your time. Get her to present in the interview for five minutes on anything, a pen, her favourite hobby or her best holiday. It does not matter what the content is, it matters how she conveys the message and how enthusiastic she is.

I read once that you should always ask a prospective salesperson about his relationship with his mother, and that if he has a great relationship, then he is more likely to be a great salesperson. I don't know how true this is but I thought I would share the wisdom as it may be correct, so use it if you like it.

Always take a salesperson on with a probation period as he may interview really well but suck out in the real world. Also if it is not working out after say, 90 days, please don't hang on desperately hoping that it will work out. Bitter experience has told me that it never does.

Cost of a Mis-Hire

This should focus your mind on hiring the right person. Below are the results of a 2006 study, so you can put the value up higher to compensate for inflation.

In Dr. Bradford Smart's 2006 study, fifty-four clients supplied data on their costs of mis-hired employees. This study was based on the belief that hiring people is an investment, so why not calculate ROIs? This survey instrument instructed the respondents to generate direct and indirect cost estimates on typical mis-hires and poor performers, not the most costly, not the least. Of the 54 respondents, more than half were division presidents or above. Some of the companies participating in this study were Motorola, General Electric, General Cable, General Signal, AlliedSignal, and Con Agra.

Cost of Mis-Hires

Total costs in hiring the person:

- Recruitment/search fees
- Outside testing, interviewing, record checking, physical exam
- HR department time
- HR department administrative costs
- Travel costs for all candidates, spouses, other executives traveling to meet candidate
- Time/expenses of non-HR people
- Relocation

Compensation: (sum for all years person was in job)

- Base $_____x number of years
- Bonuses including signing and performance bonuses
- Stock options
- Benefits
- Clubs
- Car expenses

Maintaining person in job: (sum for all years person was in job)

- Secretarial assistance
- Office rental
- Furniture, computer, equipment
- Travel
- Training

Total severance:

- Severance fee (salary, benefits, use of office)
- Outplacement counselling fee
- Costs in negotiating separation
- Costs in lawsuits caused by the person (EEOC, harassment, EPA, OSHA, etc.)
- Administrative costs in separation
- Wasted time of people in separation
- "Bad press" (loss of corporate good will, reputation)

Mistakes/failures, missed and wasted business opportunities:

"The single biggest estimable cost in mis-hiring is the wasted or missed business opportunity. For 27 years I have witnessed multimillion-dollar fiascos that clearly could have been avoided had an A player been hired instead of a C player. One of the most insidious elements of 'wasted or missed business opportunity' goes to the heart of top grading. C players hire C players and drive away A players. Several clients carefully tracked the costs of C players mis-hiring people, and the cumulative costs through an organization where there are a lot of C-player managers were astronomical." C players drive away key customers, hire other C players, impair customer loyalty, erode employee morale and trust, fail to enter new "hot" markets, fail to implement necessary measures, waste money, and drive away high performing employees.

Disruption:

Costs of inefficiency in the organization, lower morale, lower productivity, impaired teamwork. The author considers this the biggest understated cost. "More than half of the respondents registered the cost at $0. I called them to ask why, and they said assigning a dollar value of costs was too difficult, too subjective. They could ballpark all the other costs, but felt the cost of disruption would amount to a wild guess. Almost all respondents, however, indicated that they believe costs associated with disrupting the workplace are huge. C players make mistakes affecting and disrupting many people. Instead of removing business land mines, they inadvertently plant them. As the termination of a C player approaches, political jockeying takes place and more meetings waste time on internal issues, rather than on beating competitors.

The results of this study are probably conservative because many of the companies supplying the numbers are great companies. Some wrote "best practices," including those pertinent to top grading. These companies are quick to identify mis-hires and nip them in the bud. Lesser companies have more mis-hires and live with the consequences many more years. My guess is that for average companies, the costs of mis-hires are perhaps 25 times base compensation for those under $100,000 and 40 times base for those earning $100,000-$250,000.

Estimated value of contributions of the mis-hire:

Even if a $50,000-per-year store manager drove away customers and stole $1M, perhaps he contributed something---hired five excellent employees, came up with a merchandising idea worth $500K per year to the bottom line.

Maybe you will pay more attention next time you hire a person for your sales team. Frightening, isn't it?

Avoiding Brain Farts

I am constantly astonished as to the bonus structures people put in place for salespeople. How targets are set and re-evaluated and how un-motivational the whole pay structure is.

First I believe that you should never, ever set a ceiling of income for a salesperson. All they do is sandbag, stop selling and get de-motivated. Why would you want to do that, it's crazy. Allow your salespeople to earn more than you, and a good business owner allows salespeople to be the top earners in the company. As long as you make profit on everything they sell, you can only win.

Second, why not offer different packages to salespeople with different belief levels? Many years ago I was told of a very large technology company that offered three main sales packages. The first was a high basic and low commission, the second a lower basic and more commission and the third a minimal basic and a very rewarding commission structure. After several years of doing this it does not take a genius to work out that the best salespeople chose the third and earned far more than the less competent salespeople.

Even if you don't go through with it, why not offer it to a prospective sales employee and see how she reacts? Generally the ones with the most belief will pick the most chance of reward. Too high a basic allows for settling and breeds comfort. Hungry, competent salespeople are amazing and should be allowed to flourish.

Third, if your sales cycle is, let's say five months on average, then don't have monthly targets. It leads to brain farts and salespeople doing crazy things to get the deal in by the end of the month. So many deals get pressurised out of the pipeline because the salesperson feels the pressure to deliver in unrealistic timescales.

One of our suppliers' sales team is measured on monthly targets with an average sales cycle of 3-6 months. I often get a call from my account manager asking if I can pull things in early to help with the monthly target, of course I don't; I let the sale happen in its own time.

I was playing golf with a director of a large corporate company about a year ago and he said that they were just about to purchase a few million dollars' worth of IT equipment, but that he was holding out to the end of the quarter as he knew he could get a huge discount (if I remember, he said $400,000) if he waited. They were going to buy it, the sale was done and now that technology company was about to lose that much money because of inappropriate sales measurement targets.

Now I understand that it is a tricky area as you need to get the sales in, the company needs to see consistent revenue and you have targets to hit. I would suggest that you allow for your best people to be measured on a longer term view so they can sell with freedom and be allowed to flourish. If someone is new they do need to deliver to prove their worth, so a one-size-fits-all is not always appropriate.

So in conclusion, allow your team to flourish. Give them the guidance and skills they need to be more successful than you. Help them in every way you can and only hire the best you can get and reward them handsomely. Get in the trenches with them and experience the front line sales activity often so you can see what is happening out there. If you do that you will get everything you want.

Close

OK, so I have covered a lot and honestly, it has been difficult to keep a flowing structure to this book as there is so much ground to cover.

I hope you got a lot out of it and that you will be a better salesperson because of it.

In essence, to close, I hope that you adapt to the changing world and the changing needs of your audience. Educate them as much as you can and make sure that you help them with their pain and problems. Make sure that you give them amazing "wow" facts to engage initially, and then spend time educating them and helping them achieve their goals.

Be focused on the whole process of the sale, and don't give up if it starts looking like it is too hard. They need you to be there for them and help them out. They need you to know your stuff and they need you to help them look good in front of their colleagues.

Make sure that the other areas of your business look after them too. There is nothing worse than closing a sale only to have the customer support team who come in after you make a mess of it. As far as you can, keep control of their experience both as a prospect and as a client.

Remain their trusted advisor long after the sale has been done so you can retain the business and allow them to get you more business. Remember that rapport is the most important outcome for you when dealing with people, so work on it constantly and keep it going.

Keep yourself motivated, educated and in check. Look after yourself physically and emotionally, keep in shape and look smart, always!

I hope you enjoyed this book and if so please leave a great review (the last word on closing, always ask for the sale!) on the site you bought it from, it is the currency of authors and it means a lot to me. I would also love to hear from you so please check out my blog http://www.21stcenturyselling.co.uk/ and email me with any questions or success stories you have at hello@21stcenturyselling.co.uk.

Happy selling!